# RED RIVER

Originally published under the title
*Blazing Guns on the Chisholm Trail*

By
**BORDEN CHASE**

BANTAM BOOKS
NEW YORK

A BANTAM BOOK *published by arrangement with*
Random House, Inc.

Bantam Edition Published
September, 1948

Originally published under the title
*Blazing Guns on the Chisholm Trail*

Copyright, 1946, 1947, by
The Curtis Publishing Company

Copyright, 1948, by Random House, Inc.

All rights reserved under international and Pan American copyright conventions

 Bantam Books are published by Bantam Books, Inc. Its trade mark, consisting of the words "BANTAM BOOKS" and the portrayal of a bantam as here reproduced, is registered in the U. S. Patent Office.

*Printed in the United States of America*

## Printing Statement:

Due to the very old age and scarcity of this book, many of the pages may be hard to read due to the blurring of the original text, possible missing pages, missing text and other issues beyond our control.

Because this is such an important and rare work, we believe it is best to reproduce this book regardless of its original condition.

Thank you for your understanding.

*To my friend*
**DAN DILLON CASEMENT**

## CAST OF CHARACTERS

**THOMAS DUNSON:** A bull of a man, he would drive his herd to Missouri to save the State of Texas, even if it killed him.

**MATHEW GARTH:** Dunson's foreman knew when he had to take over.

**TESS MILLAY:** Green-eyed and sultry-voiced, she didn't want her man to be killed.

**CHERRY VALENCE:** He had killed twenty men and would kill many more.

**JOHN MEEKER:** Texas cattle king who was particular where his beef went.

**TEELER YACEY:** He scouted the land for Indians—and found fancy women.

**GROOT:** The cook had to make a sack of flour last ten days.

**THE DONEGAL:** He ran the Boar's Head, where he sold whiskey and wickedness.

**BUNK KENNELLY:** He started the stampede that cost two lives.

**REED ATCHISON**
**WILLIAM SUTTER**
**OLD LEATHER** } They drove the herd along the Chisholm Trail.
**BALDY McLEAN**
**BUSTER McGEE**

# 1

His name was Thomas Dunson, born in Birkenhead across the Mersey from Liverpool, come from England God knows how. A bull of a man. A brute of a man. Thick-necked, low-jowled, with eyes that looked out at you like the rounded gray ends of bullets in a pistol cylinder. And there he sat, all slumped like a bulging bag of grain on the wide seat of the Conestoga wagon. The hands that held the reins were heavy across the backs. The fingers were blunt, flat across the tips. His head rolled with the motion of the wagon as it lurched along over the flatlands.

Two mares were in the traces. Quarter mares with broad hips and heavy gaskins. Built to work; built to run. Both had been bred to the sorrel stud that followed the wagon at the end of a tie rope. Foundation stock. Dunson's eyes watched the slow, rhythmic motions of the younger mare's rump. Perhaps he was thinking of the colt she would drop in another six months. Perhaps not. Dunson's thoughts were hidden things.

Ahead, the lead wagon dipped its tongue as the team moved down the grade of a dry stream bank. One after another the following wagons answered the curve of the ground. It had been this way for days. Crawling snakelike across the face of a continent. Heading west. Always west, across mountains, rivers, stretches of desert. . . . They'd found gold in California just a year ago, heavy red gold.

Another mile and the wagon train stopped. Or rather, a portion of it stopped when Dunson checked the mares at a curve in the dry wash. Those behind him waited while a rider, dressed in leather, turned back from the lead wagon.

"Close it up!" he called. "We don't stop for another two hours."

Almost it was as though Dunson hadn't heard the words. His gray eyes looked south, reaching out over the flatlands. Again the rider called. Slowly and with reluctance Dunson turned to face the mounted man.

"I'll leave you here," he said. "My way is south."

"South . . . ?" The rider shook his head. "You'll find Indians to the south."

"I'll find water there, too. Water and grass for my bull."

Argument was in the rider's eyes. But Dunson had dropped the reins and was standing erect in the wagon. His feet were widespread, thrust hard against the floor boards as though with difficulty they held aloft the weight of muscle and flesh that made this man. He looked again toward the south. And as he did another head followed his. A horned head with a flat face—the head of Dunson's bull.

Held by a ring in its nose and a light line to the tail of the Conestoga wagon, the deep-chested animal distended its nostrils and dragged in the distant scent of grass. A wide hoof struck the earth. Sound poured from the bull's throat. Dunson nodded.

"I'll leave you here," he said again.

The wagon turned south. The rider shrugged. Others had left the wagon trains. Others had seen a pleasant valley, a cool stream. They'd turned aside. And months later men had found gray ashes, a wagon tire or two, and a rubble of picked-over bones beside the foundation of a house that was never built. . . .

South and west—morning found Dunson slouched on the seat of his wagon. Moving south and west. Slowly, suiting the pace of his mares to the plodding gate of the monstrous bull. He reached into his jacket to hunt a twist of tobacco. His mouth opened wide. The short, square teeth closed with a snap. A wrench of the powerful neck—then the ends of the twist fell unnoticed to the wagon floor.

Movement in the brush. Dunson checked the team and lifted his rifle with a single gesture. He waited. It wasn't wise to waste lead—even on an Indian. When you rode the wagons westward you waited until your sights were lined on the place where life could be stopped with a single shot.

There was a sharp, rushing snort from the tail of the wagon. Then a heavy roar as Dunson's bull gave tongue. The rifle lowered. Bewilderment came into Dunson's eyes as out of the brush stepped a teen-age boy leading a cow at the end of a rope. A boy who looked past Dunson, past the wagon.

"Hi, you!" called Dunson. "You with that cow!"

The boy turned like a dreamer in answer to some half-heard voice. He looked at Dunson with eyes that were focused on infinity.

"Where are you going with that cow?" asked Dunson.

"She's my cow." The words were ghosts of sound.

"Where are you going with her?"

"She's my cow. She got away. She's my cow."

Recognition now. Dunson had seen this boy before. Seen him in the wagon train, part of the sixth group. There had been a mother and a lean-jawed father—perhaps two older sisters. Dunson wasn't sure. He wouldn't remember the boy if it weren't for the cow. Her ribs showed from lack of grain and her hooves were worn. But she was a good cow. Good as the two that had started across the continent behind Dunson's wagon. The two that had died on the way.

"You're heading wrong," said Dunson. He pointed to the north. "The wagon train is off there."

"She's my cow," said the boy again.

The words were flat in the stillness. Dunson didn't hear them. He wasn't listening. Instead his eyes held to the distant horizon of the north where smoke lifted toward the heavens. A tall, wavering column of smoke such as might come when flames eat the canvas and wood of a wagon train. Dunson climbed from the seat. He crossed to the dazed boy.

"Indians?" he said. "Did the wagons meet Indians?"

"She's my cow. She got away. She's my cow."

Dunson slapped him across the face. The blunt fingers left marks on the cheek. The boy stared at him. Quite unconsciously the small hands doubled into fists. The small shoulders hunched forward. The corners of Dunson's mouth pulled in. Almost a smile. He slapped the boy again.

"Your cow got away," he said slowly. "You left the wagons to find her. When you got back Indians had been there."

"I didn't go back," said the boy. "Just to a hill where I could see. Everything was burning." He looked at Dunson then pointed off toward the north. "Everything was burning...."

No soft words. Not from Dunson. No friendly arm about the small shoulders. The big man studied the boy, looked at the cow. Yes, she was a good cow—as good at the two Dunson had lost. Same breed, too. She'd drop good calves.

"What's your name, boy?" asked Dunson at length.

"Mathew Garth."

"Damn it, Mathew, I've got work to do! There's no room for you. No place for you!"

"All right."

"All right, he says!" Dunson addressed his grunt to the world. "I ought to leave you here. Ought to turn my back upon you. But I won't—and like as not I'll live to regret it." He gestured toward the wagon. "Tie off your cow." And as the boy walked toward the tailgate: "Next to the stud, you idiot! Keep her away from that bull!" And, as an afterthought: "And stop your confounded bawling!"

There were tears in the eyes that stared back at Thomas Dunson. Tears that were quickly winked away. A deep breath. Mathew tied off the cow. Then, quietly: "I'm not bawling...."

They rode together. A silent man, an equally silent boy. The wheels of the Conestoga wagon turned slowly over earth that was brown and dry and hard and barren. Days grew to weeks. And there was grass. Not the lush, green, moisture-laden grass of the East. This was sterner stuff. Hardier, with grasping roots that reached down into the Texas earth and squeezed each hidden drop of moisture from the soil. Grass that was heavy with strength and life it had drawn from the Texas sun. And soon there was a river—the Rio Grande.

Thomas Dunson stopped the team near a stand of small trees. For a moment he looked about. Then he climbed down from the wagon to stand spraddled on the hard ground. He pulled a tuft of grass. He tasted it. Tasted the earth that clung to its root.

"Come down," he said to Mathew Garth.

"This is the place?"

"This is the place," said Dunson. "This is where I start. West along this river to the far hills..." His heavy arm marked a course on the distant skyline. "North to the dry stream we crossed five days past, then east again. It's mine. I take it now and I'll hold it forever."

"It's a lot of ground," said Mathew.

His eyes roamed the boundaries. Then they followed the movements of Thomas Dunson as he took a tool from the bed of the wagon and turned to the deep-chested bull. A twist of those powerful wrists and the ring came free of the animal's nose. Dunson slapped its flank. Stepped aside. The bull lumbered slowly toward the river.

"He'll go away," said Mathew.

"Anywhere he turns he'll be on my ground." Dunson jerked a wide thumb toward the mares. "Unhook the team."

Mathew obeyed. His hands were good; leather and rope liked his fingers and behaved well under them. So, too, did the mares. Each dropped her head for that quick little rub she'd come to know, each flicked a heel in answer to the slap that sent her on her way. Then Mathew's eyes grew wide as he looked to the west.

A rider was moving along the river bank toward the wagon. A pleasant man with a good smile. The horse he sat on was lean and hard. The saddle was worn. His eyes checked the men, the wagon, the stock, the equipment. His hand lifted in greeting.

"*Buenos dias, senores.* You have come a long way in that wagon."

"A long way," said Thomas Dunson. He turned from the tail gate, his heavy arms loaded with pots and tools and household ware. Carefully he set each article on the ground.

The Mexican dismounted, trailed the reins to ground-tie his horse. Again that pleasant smile: "You stay for tonight?"

"I'm going to live here," said Dunson simply.

"I am Ramon Valdez, in the employ of Don Diego Agura y Baca." Still the smile as the Mexican drew off his gloves. "In his name I bid you welcome for a night, a week, or a month. But to live here, senor, that is impossible. The ground is not for sale."

"Where is the home of Don Diego?"

Ramon gestured to the south. "Two days and two nights should take you to the hacienda." He glanced at Dunson's stud. "Although, on that horse you might better the time. He is for sale?"

Dunson ignored the question. "If I tell you I have taken this ground and mean to hold it," he said slowly, "no doubt you'll feel you must drive me off."

"What else?"

"Don't try it," said Dunson. His words were positive things. Not argumentative. "I can kill you. I don't want to but I will if you make me."

"Por Dios, you are mad!" Perplexed, the Mexican's hand hovered above his gun butt. It started downward.

*"Don't try it!"*

Ramon went for his gun. It was a fast draw, a good draw. But Dunson's huge hand flicked down. There was the sound of a single shot and smoke lifted from the barrel of his pistol. Those cold eyes looked out from beneath their heavy brows, stared down at the Mexican. Slowly Dunson put the gun away. Slowly he turned that massive head until his eyes met with those of the boy. He waited as did Mathew.

"He'll need a grave," said Dunson at long length. "There's a

Bible in the wagon, up near the water buckets. I'll read over him."

Mathew looked toward the south. "Likely there'll be others."

"Likely there will."

"You'll kill them, too?"

"If they make me," said Dunson. And he lifted his head in a faraway look. "Here I am, Mathew, and here I'll stay. On all these lands north of the river I'll grow beef. Food for the bellies of every man in our country. They'll need meat, Mathew. They can't build their cities without it." He looked off toward the squat bull near the stream edge. "Give me a score of years, Mathew. Give me a score of years and you'll see beef cattle grazing as far as your eye can reach. God knows what they'll look like—not like my bull by the water, there. Hardier, somewhat. Stringier, too, I'm afraid. But here they'll be—bulls and cows and heifers and steers. Thousands of them."

Some inner flame was at work. It heated the bullet-like eyes that swept over the boy. "My bull and your cow. My gun and you at my back. We'll build an empire, Mathew! *By God, we'll build an empire!*"

The huge hand went out; the same hand that a moment ago had killed a man. Into it went the smaller fingers of Mathew Garth. Small teeth bit against a lower lip to stifle a groan at the pressure of the grip. Dunson turned to point beyond the stand of trees. "The big house will go there. Beyond it, a barn. Then a second barn. We'll run the corrals along the river and put a bunk house on that rise of ground. . . .

## 2

A SCORE of years—mad, cruel, bitter years of conflict in which a nation trembled on the rim of ruin. War between the states. A day of defeat; heartbreak; and peace. Then a man in gray with a battle-dulled sword rode into the town of Memphis. Mathew Garth—the freckled kid who had tried to drag a cow across a continent—a man now. Tight twisted and burned to the color of Texas. Big hands and small hips. Eyes that carried the haze of early morning. Strange eyes—they'd caught the habit of looking out at you like the rounded ends of bullets in a pistol cylinder.

And there were other things that had come to this boy grown tall. Things a man learns only in war. Things Mathew had learned in the long, swift marches under Jeb Stuart; in the red swirl of battle; in the tight moments beside a fallen saddle mate; in the cruel, merciless business of keeping alive when those who look for your death are on every side.

Yes, Mathew had gone to the wars. He'd fought for the state he called his own. Now it was over and he was heading home. Riding south along the bank of the Mississippi toward Texas. Battle weary, with a single coin in the pocket of his faded gray uniform. He checked his mount on the Chickasaw bluffs and looked at the dark waters. Night had come to Memphis. The chill winds of the north walked along the river and rippled the surface. There were lights to the south—yellow lights that came from the windows of an ancient river steamer moored to a sagging dock.

Mathew was cold. He was hungry. He fingered the silver coin in his pocket then walked his horse toward the dock.

Music came from the lighted windows, music and laughter and the shouts of men. Mathew read the name painted in gold along the rotted hull—the *River Palace*. Too old to work, her engines rusted and long since dead, she now served as a place where gamblers went to win the gold of drunken men while river bawds danced to help them at their trade

But there was food in the *River Palace*. Mathew tethered his horse where the broken wall of a shack took the bite from the wind. He eased the cinch. Then he walked up the sagging gangway and into the glare of the main saloon. Oil flames danced in a hundred lamps. There were men at the tables and men at the long carved hardwood bar. Women in dresses that showed their legs. Hard-faced, brittle, laughing women who flaunted the thing they had for sale.

Mathew found a table well back from a lamplit stage where two fiddles screamed and a man blew a horn. A Negro came to his elbow. Mathew ordered sowbelly and coffee. He paid with his coin and ate slowly and thoroughly when the food was set before him. Noise and laughter swirled about his shoulders. Perfumes that were dank and heavy and sold by the dark merchants of New Orleans lifted to blend with the harsh scent of whiskey. The place smelled of sweat and humanity.

Then a woman stepped onto the stage. A golden woman with clear white skin and eyes the color of ancient jade. A tall woman, cold in her manner, with a glance that was filled with the scorn of men. Therissa Millay—Tess of the River, out of the Southland to set men mad in Jackson and Natchez, Cairo and St. Louis, and now in the city of Memphis.

The laughter stopped. The noise grew small. Then the fiddles played and the woman sang. Mathew set down his cup. And as he listened the voice built a picture of a finer world—a pleasant place where there was no war, where the sun was warm and the breezes soft, where women were kind and the days were long. Then she sang in French and the words were strange, but again the story was clear. It told of women with soft round arms, with lips that were moist and eyes that smiled, and it cautioned all men that life was a coin, gone forever once it was spent.

And as she sang those green eyes drifted slowly about the crowded room, passing like a hurrying shadow across the upturned faces. They met with those of Mathew Garth and for an instant they paused. Why? What held them there? As well ask why Mathew's hands gripped hard on the table edge. An instant, no longer, then the song was through and the singer was gone.

There was shouting. Cheers and cries and the sound of rough hands beating together to tell of their owners' pleasure. They wanted more and they called for more. But the song was over and when once again Tess stepped from the curtains it was to leave the stage and come down onto the floor of the crowded saloon.

Men stood and offered empty chairs. They offered drinks and rippled piles of gold coins between their fingers. Tess smiled and walked between them or around them, pausing once to nod a greeting to a dark-faced man in a beaver hat with rings on his fingers and a stone in his scarf. Then she walked to the table where Mathew was seated and looked at the empty chair beside him.

"May I?" she said.

"It's kind of you," he said quietly. "It's more than kind but I've spent my last coin."

The green eyes narrowed as Tess let them wander slowly over the tattered gray uniform, the tarnished scabbard and heavy gun that hung in a work-worn holster. Then she seated herself unasked at the table and the trace of a smile grew on her lips.

"I hardly expected you'd be carrying gold in that uniform," she said. "And you might be wise to find some clothes of another color, now that your cause is lost."

"I like this color," said Mathew.

"So do I," said Tess. "And for some strange reason I like the man who wears it. What is your name?"

"Mathew Garth of Texas."

"You're going home?"

"Yes."

"What's waiting for you there?"

"Work," said Mathew. "Other than that I don't know."

"Tell me about yourself."

"There's little to tell. I'd rather hear about you."

Tess laughed and shook her head when a waiter paused with an inquiring glance. "Would you like to know why I came to your table?"

"Yes."

"Because once long ago a man like you taught me to read and taught me to spell," said Tess. "He was a good man. If he'd lived he'd have worn the uniform you wear. His eyes would have been clear and clean and honest as yours. He was the one man in life I've ever respected. I called him father."

"Thank you," said Mathew.

'And now," said Tess as her manner changed, "why don't you ask what a nice girl like me is doing in a place like this?"

"I figure it's none of my business."

As he spoke, a thin man in gambler's clothes crossed the room toward them. Tess looked sharply at Mathew. "Neither is this," she said. "Keep your hand off your gun and your mouth closed."

The thin man stood at the table. Frenchy DeLonge, up from New Orleans with a reputation that was sharp as the slant of his eyes. Gambler, killer, wanted on the Gulf for a hundred crimes. He tapped a slim hand against Tess' shoulder and nodded toward the stage.

"Go back to your room," he said sharply. "Stay there until I send for you. Do it now!"

"Why?"

"Because I tell you to!"

"Or is it because the Donegal is coming to pay you a call?" said Tess. Her smile was as cold as the words.

"Do as I tell you," said Frenchy. His thin fingers curled

about the woman's wrist and tightened to bruise the skin.

Mathew's leg pushed back his chair. His hands moved across the table top toward the edge. Tess looked at him, a fast glance filled with warning. Then she turned to look toward the door where a giant of a man stood etched against the outer darkness. His great red beard flamed in the yellow light of the lamps. His dark eyes sparkled and snapped as he looked slowly about a room that had suddenly grown quiet. A table stood in his way. He brushed it aside with a heavy hand that carried chairs and men along as it crashed.

"So there ye are!" he cried. And his voice was deep as the bellow of a bull. "Tess, girl—what are you doing in this filthy nest when the Donegal has offered you marriage? If it's money you want instead of me love, there's work aplenty at the Boar's Head where I sell both whiskey and wickedness!"

Frenchy's hand lifted from the woman's wrist. He moved to place the width of a table between himself and the oncoming giant. Tess looked again at Mathew who was standing. Her head moved ever so slightly, warning him to silence, warning against any move of his hand toward the gun in the worn holster. Mathew waited.

The Donegal barged across the floor, sweeping tables and men aside as he moved with the surge of the avalanche. Facing Tess, he lifted a blunt forefinger to tap it lightly against the woman's cheek.

"Go fetch your bonnet an' put on your shawl," he said. The words rode on the crest of a monstrous laugh. "Pack up your duds and give me your trunk, you're movin' this instant to the Boar's Head."

"She's staying here," said Frenchy DeLonge.

"The devil you say!" laughed the Donegal. He turned again to Tess. "Do as I tell you, woman, or I'll paddle you over me knee!"

"She's staying here," said Frenchy again. "And you're leaving."

"Am I, now?" cried the Donegal. "Then if I am, 'tis only

to carry your filthy carcass to the end of the dock and flick it into the river!"

He reached one heavy hand toward the gambler, then drew it back as a thin blade drew blood from his wrist. There was a mad bellow of rage. Frenchy stepped in, moving his feet with the smooth ease of a dancer. Again the slim blade drew blood, this time from the cheek of the Donegal. Frenchy leaped back then circled quickly, testing with the knife tip for a place where life was close to the surface and could be stolen away with the twist of a blade.

Another quick stroke, then the Donegal's great hand caught the gambler's wrist. Frenchy was drawn forward into the terrible grip of two monstrous arms. The Donegal's head went down. Like some gigantic bear that has caught its prey, he locked his arms about the gambler's waist. The arms tightened. Again and again the knife ripped quickly at flesh and bone and sinew. Still the Donegal squeezed, one hand in the other, his chin pressed firmly against the gambler's chest.

Frenchy screamed. A gasping, strangling cry that burst from his tortured lungs. A rib cracked. Then another. The vice that was built of bone and muscle drew tighter. Always tighter. A hard-faced man in the crowd cursed and turned away. A woman sobbed. Another cried out in protest. Still the arms drew in. There was the grinding crackle of bones that are twisted and torn in their sockets. Frenchy DeLonge grew limp. His back was broken and his life was gone.

"Fetch your bonnet, Tess," said the Donegal. He dropped the thing he held in his arms. "Fetch your bonnet and we'll be leavin' this place."

"You're a fool, Donegal," said Tess quietly. "You're a great red fool. Now get in there and pack my trunk."

The Donegal laughed. And as though there were no blood flowing from a dozen wounds he marched across the floor toward the rooms behind the stage. Tess turned to the silent man beside her.

"Good-bye, Mathew," she said. "You've finished your meal

and the night is young. I'd hurry along to Texas if I were you."

"Perhaps you're right," said Mathew.

"I'm sure I'm right," said Tess. She offered a hand that was smooth and small and very white. "Until our next meeting..."

Mathew took the small hand within his own. "I've work to do in Texas. I doubt that we'll meet again."

"I *know* we'll meet again," said Tess. Her fingers curled tightly against his. "Somehow—for some strange reason, Mathew, I know we'll meet again."

She took back her hand, turned and hurried across the floor. Mathew watched her go. He looked at the ring of frightened faces about him, glanced once at the thing on the floor and crossed to the door. The wind that swept south along the river was good. Its taste was fresh and clean and sharp on a man's tongue. Mathew tightened the worn cinch under his horse. He stepped into the saddle and swung south along the Mississippi.

# 3

As Dunson had promised a score of years before, a big house had been built beyond the clump of trees. Built of stone and hand-hewn timbers. Beyond it a barn. Then a second barn. Corrals stretched out along the Rio Grande and smoke lifted from the chimney of the bunk house. Thomas Dunson was there. Older now, he stood in the half light of morning, his feet spread wide, thrust hard against a rise of earth. And his eyes looked out over the tossing horns of five thousand head of cattle.

Lean cattle, stringy beasts with gigantic horns. More than half wild. Riders hazed the distant fringes of the herd. Others carried war bags from the bunk house and tossed them into a pair of high-wheeled ox carts. Low-waisted men with no meat on their rumps. Shaggy men, themselves as wild as the beasts they herded. Each wore a gun.

Another group was at work beside a branding chute, running the long wavering road brand on the flanks of the last batch brought in. Smoke from a wood fire mingled with the dust. A mad-eyed steer lunged against the chute end.

"Another Diego!" called the brander.

"Turn him loose," said Mathew.

Yes, Mathew was home from the wars. He'd reached Texas to find his homeland starving, a little bewildered but not beaten. Not frightened. Confused, rather, at the thing that had happened here and was still happening. Confused to find that the State of Texas was dying. And so were her sons.

Starved out, with a million tons of beef on the hoof drifting across a quarter million square miles of worthless ground. Preyed upon by Northern carpetbaggers. Harried by the dreamers in Congress. Left to rot under a golden sun that could bring them everything except hard, cold cash of the realm. Such was Texas after the war.

Lesser men would have turned away. Lesser men *did* turn away. Thomas Dunson stayed. Who knows how he kept alive? Who knows how he held his herds together? But he did. And when the lean, tired men straggled south from the battlefields Dunson gave each a bed, a handful of food from his meager store, a horse to ride and a rope to throw. Then he put them to work to bring in his cattle. Sent them into the valleys and draws to round up a herd of five thousand head.

"There's a market in Missouri," he said to Mathew when the tall man came home to the ranch. "I'll drive to it, Mathew. In spite of Congress and carpetbaggers, I'll drive these cows to market!"

The roundup was finished. The road brand was searing into the hides of the last bunch brought in. Today they would start the drive.

"Another Diego!" called the brander.

"Turn him loose," said Mathew again. And the man at the chute gate reached for the bar that would free the steer.

"Hold that!" Thomas Dunson left the rise of ground and walked slowly toward the man with the iron. He punched a blunt thumb toward the steer. "Put a road brand on him."

"He's a Diego," said the brander—Teeler Yacey, long-boned and poverty thin, with a limp that grew when a Northern cavalry saber cut through his hip.

"Put a road brand on him."

Mathew pointed to the crude, sprawling brand of the Diego's plain on the rump of the steer. Teeler's right. It's a Diego steer."

"I don't see the Diego brand," said Dunson.

His eyes moved from the steer to find Mathew's, and hold there. Gray on gray, both misted with a translucent curtain. Challenge in Dunson's—cold, purposeful challenge. And in Mathew's an answer to the challenge. No spoken words. But a battle was being fought. The man at the chute gate knew it.

So did Teeler Yacey who held the running iron loosely in his gloved hands and waited.

"I don't see the Diego brand," said Dunson again.

Mathew shrugged. He nodded to Teeler: "Put the iron on him."

Just that. Nothing more. Teeler ran the iron in a wavering line along the steer's flank. The great beast bawled; lunged at the gate. The bar snapped back and a rider hazed the steer toward the herd. A second was branded. Then a third went into the chute.

"Another Meeker!" called Teeler.

"I don't see the Meeker brand," said Dunson quietly.

This, without a glance toward the chute. Dunson's eyes were steady on Mathew. The heavy head was drawn down hard on the blocky man's neck. A moment passed. Dunson's lower lip thrust forward. Teeler waited. So did the man on the gate.

"Put the iron on him," said Mathew quietly. He turned away from the chute and stepped into his saddle. "Put the iron on *all* of them."

"I'll have a word with you, Mathew." Dunson crossed toward the rise of ground. "Yes, I'll have a word with you."

Mathew followed, suiting the pace of his stud to the rolling gait of Thomas Dunson. When the owner paused Mathew didn't step down. Instead, he waited, one forearm resting on the pommel of his worn saddle. Men of the West have a name for the fortunate few who fit well on the back of a stallion. They call them "stud horse men." Such was Mathew Garth. A male creature, loaded with threat in every movement. Equal to the task of mastery over a mount that was half horse, half tiger. He looked silently down at Dunson.

"The army's spoiled you, Mathew," said the owner. "Spoiled you to the point where at times you forget I am the master of this spread."

"I don't forget."

"See that you don't," said Dunson. He gestured toward the

herd. "Those beasts out there are worthless as long as they stay in the State of Texas. We've lost a war and lost our market. Diego, Meeker and the rest of these fools would take a dollar a head, fifty cents, a quarter—any coin that's made of silver! I'll be hanged if I will. Not for my beef. Not while there's a market in Missouri. Not while Northern buyers will pay twenty dollars at the rail head!"

"We've got no argument along those lines."

"We've got no argument along *any* lines," said Dunson.

"There are quite a few *strays* in that herd. Meeker might not like to see our road brand on some of them."

"I'll argue that with Meeker."

"Now might be a good time," said Mathew. "He's coming your way."

Dunson turned to see an ancient Texan riding toward them. White hair long on his collar, a flowing mustache and a face cut with deep lines, John Meeker sat his horse with the ease sixty years in the saddle gives a man. Beside him rode a younger man, dark, amused, glancing about with a casualness that was more that casual. Both checked their mounts at the rise of ground.

"See you're goin' to make the drive," said Meeker

"That's right," said Dunson.

"Got news yesterday about Cummerlan. He drove three thousand head clear to the Missouri border before they jumped him. Killed all his men, took all his cattle. Said they had the law with 'em."

"Law?"

Meeker nodded. "Said his steers would bring Texas fever to the Northern cattle."

"What's this rubbish about Texas fever?"

"I don't know," said Meeker. "Just another excuse for the border gangs to steal Texas beef. They've run off with two hundred thousand head up to now, and not one silver dollar has come back to Texas; only a few of the drivers."

"So you'd advise me not to make the drive?"

"It's not my business to advise," said Meeker quietly. He looked thoughtfully toward the cattle. "Must be five thousand threes and fours in that herd. For a man who has only been in Texas twenty-odd years you seem to do good without any advice."

"Yes, I do good," said Dunson. Again that lower lip jutted forward. "I'm going to keep on doing good while the rest of you cattlemen sit around and watch yourselves go broke. You're licked. I'm not. I'll drive my beef to market and all hell won't stop me!"

"Do what you want with *your* beef," said Meeker slowly. "But I'm sort of particular where *my* beef goes. Mind if I have a look at that herd?"

"I do mind."

"You'd try to stop us?" This from the younger man.

"Who're you?" asked Dunson.

"Cherry Valance, up from Valverde."

Cherry Valance—and a mad pair of devils danced in the pupils of those dark eyes. Cherry Valance; and the rider laughed at the reaction to the name. A strange laugh that lifted through four notes of the octave. Irritating to a man, attractive to women. It matched the smile that was both charming and impudent. Matched the attitude of this mad son of Texas who had killed twenty men "not counting the Yankees he fought in the war."

All of Texas knew the name; knew this weird product of a Louisiana French father and a Basque mother. From Matagorda to the Red River, from Beaumont to the Pecos—and there were many who lived south of the Rio Grande who could tell of this dark rider with the shiny hair that twisted into curls at the rim of his forehead. Danger rose with the man. It lived in his eyes, in his musical laugh, in the deceptive swing of his back as he bent forward in a little bow of introduction. It was hidden in the small, delicately formed almost feminine hand that was held in an inquisitive gesture not too many inches above his gun butt.

"You'd try to stop us?" he asked again.

"I would," said Mathew.

Cherry turned to look down the barrel of the gun Mathew held at his hip. The barrel was still. Stone steady. No use to gamble, although for an instant the thought lived in Cherry's eyes. Instead, he laughed and crossed his forearms on the pommel.

"Damn it all, Mathew—put that gun away!" said Dunson. And without a glance to verify the order he moved in to tap a square finger against Meeker's knee. "All right, John—there's a few of your steers in that herd. Some with Diego's brand on them. None of you have held a roundup in three years. Your cows are scattered over ten thousand square miles and you haven't money to hire riders to bring them in." He indicated the men near the herd. "My last silver went into wages for this roundup—that and food for our drive to Missouri. Yes, we've brought in some of your stock. I haven't time to cut it from the rest. But I'll drive it to Missouri and give you two dollars a head when I get back.'

"*If* you get back," said Meeker, and he grinned.

"That's your gamble."

"I like it," said Meeker at long length. "And sometimes— sometimes I like you, Dunson. You're a strange man. But maybe that's because you're an Englishman."

"Maybe it's because I'm a Texan."

"That," said Meeker after thought, "is open to question." He turned to his companion. "Come along, Cherry."

"I'll stay a while." Cherry lifted a hand in a friendly good-bye as Meeker rode off, then turned to the others. "Thought you might need another man on the drive."

"Sorry," said Mathew. "We're full up."

Cherry's eyes twinkled. "I'd like to hear that from Dunson."

"You heard it from his segundo. We're full up."

"One moment, Mathew," said Dunson. He measured Cherry with an appraising glance. "They say this man is good with a gun." And then to Cherry: "Is that true?"

"I manage to keep alive."

"You might find it more difficult along the Missouri border."

"I might, at that."

"Wages ten dollars a month," said Dunson abruptly. "Triple that if the steers bring better than fifteen dollars a head at the railroad. If we lose the herd you lose your wages."

"Suits me."

"One thing more. A man who signs for this drive *finishes* the drive. No quitting along the way."

"Then I take it I'm hired." Cherry turned those mad eyes toward Mathew. "Where do I ride?"

"On point," said Mathew quietly.

"On point . . . ?" Cherry echoed the words in surprise. "I thought that was reserved for your best riders."

"I figure you to be my best rider."

"I don't understand."

"Is that important?" said Mathew. He turned to Dunson. "Any further orders?"

Dunson shook his head then swung a blunt hand to indicate the herd. "Take them to Missouri, Mathew."

Just that. No handclasp. No ceremony. "Take them to Missouri, Mathew," and Dunson turned his broad back on the herd that must travel a thousand miles to market.

A thousand miles! And a thousand deaths. Coyotes and wolves, and men with the habits of both. Torrents and gales and rivers in flood, badlands, dry wells, stampedes—ten miles a day, fifteen with luck. But there was a market in Missouri—a market for beef. What difference if the graves of two hundred drivers marked the trails? What difference if two hundred thousand Texas steers had been scattered and stolen? There was a market in Missouri!

Mathew motioned to Teeler Yacey: "Move them along . . . !"

A rider near the bunk house caught the words. He answered with a high, wild, lifting call that ended with the staccato sharpness of the coyote's cry. He ran to his horse and stepped into the saddle. Promptly, the horse dropped its head and broke in two. "Hi . . . !" called the rider, and raked a shoulder with a long rowelled spur. "Hi-yaaa! We're off to Missoura-hi-yaaaa . . . !"

Other riders turned their mounts toward the herd. Two high-wheeled wagons rolled, bucketing and bumping slowly over the hard ground. A lean cook with long hair waved to the riders. He cracked his bull whip at Teeler who cursed him blue. Cheerfully the cook cursed back. Dust lifted in a sullen cloud. The great beasts stirred.

Movement in the herd. Slow, almost imperceptible. It rippled along the rim like the first swelling lift of a giant wave. Bending outward. Heaving, breathing, filled with the irresistible force that is found in countless tons of muscle and flesh. Frightening in its immensity. Moving north and east toward the morning sun. Held in movement by the constant herding of thirty men.

This was the drive. Mathew and Cherry, acting as pointers, swung out the lead steers, easing them into line at the tip of a crescent that seemed to form of its own accord. Flankers and swing men moved into place, guiding the monstrous long-horned beasts into a loosely built trail herd. Four, five hundred yards across, thinning as the point moved out, broken in places with gaps that closed as the drag men urged the stragglers forward.

"Hi-yaaa! Git along little dogies . . ." And once again Texas beef started for the Missouri market. Long horns rattled and clashed, cleft hooves cut into the dry earth; there was a bawling and lunging—hides ripped with the needle-sharp points as the herd adjusted itself to driving space. Then the crackle of sharper, finer hooves as Bunk Kennelly brought up the remuda.

Mathew gave way at point to Teeler Yacey. He turned to run a quick glance over the remuda. Three hundred shaggy mustangs picked from the thousand-odd head that grazed on Dunson's range. Cutting horses, ropers, broncs, and "last year's broncs," each with a name given by the wrangler, and usually with a disposition to match. Sail Away Blue, Red Hell, Lightnin', Big Enough, Stinker, Straight Edge, Cannon Ball, Crawfish, Few

Brains, Gray Whizzer, Lonesome—and sometimes the men wondered if Bunk would ever run short.

Mathew dropped past the swing and rode into the dust of the drag. Here, as the drive moved on, would be found the lame, the weak and the misfit—meat for the cook fires. And here, too, was Old Leather Monte, born on the Pecos at the turn of the century, still straight in the saddle and loaded with wisdom.

His watery blue eyes cut through the dust cloud to watch the work of the raw riders assigned to the drag. Buster McGee, freckled and thin with hair that flamed like the morning sun— a nice kid in his late teens, "off for Missoura t'see the elephant." And there was Laredo Downs from Uvalde—quiet, serious, given to long silences and dark moods of thought; laughing Tom Kinney from the Corazones; Andres and Lovelock and other sons of Texas. They turned their horses against the stragglers, urging them on. And always and ever the dust of the drag billowed about their unfortunate heads.

Thinned out, the drive moved north and east across the range, winding like a giant brown snake. Mathew circled it once then joined Cherry Valance on point. For a time both rode in silence

"Likely you're wondering," said Mathew at length, "why I didn't want you on the drive."

"Didn't . . . ?" laughed Cherry. "Or still don't?"

"Dunson hired you," said Mathew. "That's good enough for me. But maybe you'd like to know why I was against it."

"Maybe I would."

"I know you by name—know you for a rider, cattleman and gun fighter."

"Thanks," said Cherry, and the mad lights danced in his eyes. "It's the last that bothers you?"

"Yes."

"You're not afraid of me."

"No, I'm not afraid of you, Cherry. Just worried about you."

Mathew half turned in his saddle to look at the herd. "You know what happens if this drive doesn't get to the market?"

Again the laugh that ran through four notes of the octave. "We lose our wages, according to Dunson."

"And what happens to Texas?"

"I don't understand."

"You're a Texan, Cherry," said Mathew. "You've ridden, as I have, from the Pecos to the Sabine. And what did you see . . . ? Stock roaming wild, ranchers roasting grain and calling it coffee, Yankee carpetbaggers grabbing land with both hands, men who fought with you during the war trying to swap a four-year steer for a half sack of flour. I asked these men to make the drive with us—asked them to try for the market in Missouri. They shook their heads. Said it can't be done."

"You know what I think?" said Cherry seriously. "I think they're right." And as Mathew looked at him in astonishment, Cherry continued: "I've ridden the border—crossed the Nations and Arkansas clear to Kansas City. They've got a hundred men for every one of yours. You'll never get through."

"We've got to get through."

"Why?" said Cherry. He rapped his knuckles irritably against the pommel of his saddle. "Why drive five thousand steers to Missouri when there's a market in Kansas?"

"Since when?"

"Since—now, I guess. I met a man. He told me the railroad was going through to a town called Abilene. Said there'd be cattle pens and a stockyard."

"An honest man?"

"I found him to be," said Cherry. "Told me the rails were fifty miles west of Kansas City. I rode out, and there they were."

"You saw the rails?"

"Almost to Topeka."

"And Abilene's further west?"

"West and south—maybe a hundred miles, so the man says."

"You didn't see Abilene?"

Cherry shook his head and those mad eyes knew laughter

again. "Had to get back to Memphis. There was a girl there. ... Do you like girls, Mathew?"

"Some girls."

"You'd like Tess of the River. Her hair is the color of Mexican gold when you hold it under the light of a lamp. And she sings, Mathew; sings for Frenchy DeLonge at the *River Palace* in Memphis. There was a rainy night when I rode in with my troop . . ."

But Mathew wasn't listening. His eyes studied the tips of his sorrel stud's ears while his mind rode out over the unborn trail that led to the Great Plains and beyond. A market for beef in Kansas . . . ?

A week on the trail; seven days of driving and the herd was bedded down for the night beyond the south branch of the Concho. Seven days during which the monstrous beasts had "walked with the grass," straggling along singly or in pairs, at times ten abreast. Long days and short nights. Dunson had set a hard pace, anxious to shake down the herd and make it trail wise quickly. Now a wood fire burned between the wagons a half mile from the bed grounds. There was the smell of sizzling beef. Groot Nadine, the long-haired cook, sampled the brew that passed for coffee. He nodded to the men near the fire.

"Drink it if y'can," he said in disgust. "Nature an' me, we done our best. But y'can't make this stuff taste good no matter if you be the best cook in Texas!"

"Why don't you try using coffee instead of grain?" said Teeler Yacey. His strong teeth tore a strip of beef and he stretched one leg to ease the ache in his hip. "An' while you're at it, mix a little more flour with the water so you get more bread."

"All right!" said Groot. *"All right!* So the bread is short an' the coffee is bad. Is that my fault? Dunson says we drive a hundred days. We got ten sacks of flour. One sack for ten days. You want to drive them last few weeks with no bread?"

"Ten sacks of flour?" said Teeler. He looked in doubt toward

Old Leather Monte, boss of the drag, who was methodically teasing his bowie blade through a slab of beef—"chewing with his knife" before he let his digestive juices finish the job.

"Ten sacks, eh?" said Monte. He shook his ancient head.

"An' less'n that of beans!" added Groot. "You'll chew beef an' drink water from the Red to Missouri if I ain't careful!"

There was a murmur of voices. Short rations were common in Texas since the war. Short rations and long hours. But this was more than short. Dunson had promised ten dollars a month and food. Ten sacks of flour wasn't food. And a man couldn't live on beef alone.

"I don't like it," said Teeler. "Dunson should've told us we were on starvation rations."

There was movement in the darkness beyond the circle of firelight. A blocky shadow, then heavy steps—each foot set deliberately before the other. Dunson stepped in to stand beside the coffee boiler. He filled a cup. Sipped the hot brew.

"What's this Dunson should have told you?" he asked quietly.

"That we're drivin' on poverty short rations," said Teeler. "It's not that I'm objectin', but there's things I like to know."

"You know it now."

"Yes—a week out on the drive."

Dunson simply looked down at Teeler. Then that lower lip jutted. A breath whistled in through the flared nostrils. "Teeler, I don't like your tone. I don't like your words." And as Teeler put aside his plate and prepared to stand: "Stay where you are!"

Something in the words stopped Teeler's movement. The lank ex-cavalryman looked up at the gray eyes above him. "I can draw from here, if that's what you mean."

"Don't try it, Teeler," said Dunson. "You're a good man. Don't make me kill you."

Tenseness came to the group at the fire. Hard men working at a hard trade. Men who had to be hard to keep alive. They'd met their share of brutal bosses—met their share of killers. This was different. Here was a man who had built a situation to force a oint. If he had to, Dunson would kill Teeler Yacey. Every man : the fire knew it. So did Teeler.

"What is it you want?" said Teeler slowly.

"The obedience I learned as a boy aboard a British man 'war," said Dunson. "This much I'll tell you and nothing more —you've got a thousand miles of trail. Short rations. Bad coffee. .t the end, a gang of border ruffians who will make you fight very inch of the way to the market." Dunson spread his legs 'ider; swept his bullet-gray eyes over the men. "I can take you 1rough. I *mean* to take you through. But by God and his rophets—I've got to have obedience to do it!"

There was silence save for the snap and crackle of the flames ; they crept along the dry wood. Silence, save for the murmur of 1e herd and an occasional protest from a troubled steer. Silence —and a low, musical laugh that lifted four notes through the ctave.

Then the voice of Cherry Valance: "I like what the man 1ys."

Dunson turned abruptly, motioned to Mathew and walked to 'here two saddled horses stood ground-tied. Both guided the orses past the litter of gear spread near the wagons and rode )ward the herd. Bunched in an irregular circle, a quarter mile 1rough at its widest point, the great beasts slept. Guards cir- led the rim, riding in pairs, singing softly the melancholy tunes 1en have crooned to cattle since the first herd was bunched.

Darkness covered the world. It crowded in from the far hori- ons, sharpened by the myriad pinpoints of star glitter in the 1ble vault of the heavens. Loneliness—a loneliness such as was ommon only to primitive man, crouched in his cave or huddled lose beside a fire. A fear-filled loneliness. And through it rode )unson and Mathew Garth—two shadows moving in a sea of ight.

"Cherry Valance tells me," said Mathew, "they're building a ailroad across Kansas. Says there'll be cattle yards at Abilene."

"That's a town?"

"A hundred and fifty miles south and west of Kansas City. It might be we could swing north when we cross the Red and head for Kansas."

"Forget it," said Dunson.

"I've ridden some of that ground," said Mathew quietly. "There's grass in the Nations and the Cherokee Strip. Good grass—enough to feed the buffalo." A moment while the horses walked quietly beside the sleeping cattle. "Once I saw a buffalo herd; it moved across the plains far as a man's eye could reach. There was no counting them." Again a moment of silence, "Where they went, we can drive cattle."

"We'll drive to Missouri."

"If we drive north through the Nations and west of the Arkansas there'll be two hundred miles between us and the border gangs. Might be we could slip past without a fight."

"If they want fight we'll give it to them."

"Fighting isn't good. Killing isn't good," said Mathew quietly. "I had to do both. I didn't like it."

"We'll drive to Missouri," said Dunson flatly. "And I'll hear no more about Kansas."

Silence again; dark silence that was made more intense by the plaintive crooning of the night hawks. Dunson and Mathew circled the herd and stopped by the wagons. The fire was down; glowing embers that pulsed under the light breeze then grayed to ashes. Mathew slipped from his mount and uncoiled his riata. Dunson did the same. No pulled saddle and slipped bridle these first weeks on the trail. Each man of the drive slept with a riata about his wrist and the end looped on the saddle horn. Always it was his best mount. Always the horse was clear of the wagon gear. A hat for a pillow and the ground for his bed, a blanket or tarp to keep out the chill of the night.

Mathew slept. The sorrel stud drooped its head. Two hours, three, then wakefulness came when the herd, following the strange custom of all cattle, stirred at midnight. Why, there is no telling. But always and ever since the dawn of creation cattle in herds have stood erect at midnight. They look about, take a dozen steps, then wearily bed down again.

A wary moment on the drive. A dangerous moment. The mournful song of the guards grew an edge of tension. "Sleep, cow, sleep. . . . I got a girl in Memphis town; sleep, cow, sleep. . ." And Mathew stirred in his blanket. Stirred and listened as little Bunk Kennelly, the wrangler, crossed to his mount to ride out for a look-see.

Half asleep, tired, stumbling in the darkness, Bunk stepped into the worn saddle. A leather thong broke. Just a small thong, but it held the mouth of his gun boot in place. The ancient Sharps slid out of the boot. A shot bucketed through the stillness as the stock jarred against the hard earth.

One shot—but it leaped through the night like a live thing. A steer snorted. Then another. Sudden movement. And the herd crashed into action. Lunging, bellowing, fear-crazed beasts! Long horns rattling and the rumble of hooves. Instant action. With one accord the entire herd started in a mad rush toward the horizon. Countless tons of muscle and flesh spilling like an avalanche across the dark earth.

"*Stampede!*" The wild cry of a rider.

No need for warning. Each man was on his feet and running. The slow were whipped erect by the tug of the riata fastened to the saddle horn. No time to look about. No time to think. Mathew leaped to the back of his stud. The reins hung free. He bent forward, knees pressing to keep his seat. Horse and rider became one. They breathed alike, moved in rhythm. One mad leap and then another. Stampede!

# 4

DUNSON and Teeler, Cherry and Old Leather raced along before the oncoming horde. Heads down, arms swinging free, they made no attempt to guide their mounts. Run, horse! Run! Miss the holes and keep running. Don't look. Don't breathe. Run! And behind you comes a tidal wave of horns and heads and hooves and muscle. Run! And the rumble of thunder runs with you.

A hundred yards. Two hundred. Nothing on four legs can equal the blinding speed the cow horse can show at this distance. Three hundred—four! Now Mathew lifted his head to glance quickly over his shoulder. A black sea of horns and heads. Mathew's feet found the stirrups. One hand lifted the reins. Still no attempt to guide the stud. Run, horse! Run! Another hundred yards and another quick glance. The stud was quartering across the face of the herd. Reaching for the far end.

"Good man," whispered Mathew.

They reached the tip of the crescent. Of his own accord the stud checked his run to the speed of the brown beasts beside him. Mathew's gun was out. It flared in the night. Again and again—firing and loading. Spinning flame into the eyes of the nearer beasts; crowding them over; starting the turn.

Another gun splashed flame. Teeler Yacey was riding low along the neck of his horse, crowding the steers, trying to turn them. Slowly a wave grew at the rim. A heaving, pulsing wave that built in pressure. Other riders emptied their guns; slashed at the steers' faces with coiled ropes; yelling, screaming men who rode like demons on the skirt of a thunder storm.

Cherry Valance was on the far side, laughing as he rode;

firing as he rode. Behind him were Dunson and Old Leather. They sensed the wave that had started in the herd. Slowly they gave way. Another wave moved across the racing beasts. Mathew was turning them; Mathew and Teeler and Laredo Downs, the quiet man from Uvalde—they were turning the herd, or a part of the herd, easing it into a giant circle. Other riders caught the drift. They strung along the edge of the herd, crowding, driving, giving definite direction to the turn.

A bunch split out, hurled from the mass like a planet that is born from the sun. No use to follow. No time. A second bunch —then a third. The riders held to the main herd, turning one horn of the crescent while the men on the far side gave way. An hour was gone—an hour made of minutes that lasted through eternity. The lead steers looked ahead to see the drag. The circle was complete. But still it moved. Around and around. Crowded, bunched, driven by the men who had long since screamed away their voices. Around and slower, like a dull black star that circles in space and dies as it loses momentum. Around and slower, and soon the stragglers stumbled to a halt.

Tired riders drooped in their saddles. Tired horses filled their lungs and emptied them with long, sighing breaths. A laugh sounded in the darkness; a mad, musical laugh that lifted through four notes. Another answered. A dozen men laughed. Twenty men. No one knew why.

Dunson detailed men to ride guard. An easy job now; the beasts had had their run. Mathew made a silent tally—one, two, Old Leather on the end, four, five, six, Cherry Valance riding ahead, eight, nine—and on to twenty-seven. Twenty-seven and they had been thirty. Others were counting. Each was silent when he completed his tally. Each paused to look as he passed a trampled mass of bone and hide and blood and flesh. Only a steer. A weak one that went down. Then another.

"Hold it," said Mathew at length. He reined his stud and pointed toward the ground. "Was it Dan Lattimer wore check pants?"

No answer for a time. Others looked down. Most looked

away. At length Teeler Yacey nodded. "Dan was riding a buckskin mare. I'd say that was the mare over there."

"And that's Dan," said Laredo Downs. "Some of him."

"What do we do?" asked Groot, the cook.

"There's a Bible in the wagon," said Dunson evenly. "I'll read over him in the morning. Nothing we can do now. Move along."

"I'll stay," said Laredo. And as he spoke there was the long, high cry of a coyote—a cry that crackled out of the darkness. "I'll stay..." said Laredo again.

The others rode on. Twice more a rider dropped from the group to sit his horse in the darkness beside a thing on the ground that had once been a saddlemate. Then camp, where a litter of torn canvas, spilled flour and splintered wood told that one of the ox carts had gone down under the tidal wave.

Dunson poked among the ruins. At length he lifted a torn Bible and shook dust from the pages. He seated himself on the tongue of the second cart and rested an elbow on his knee. Groot stirred the ashes of the fire. Tonight the men would need coffee...

In the morning the great beasts stirred to wakefulness. The riders, save for the guard, stood uncovered beside three flat graves while Dunson read: "Man that is born of woman, hath but a short time to live, and is full of misery..." Then back to camp for a lean breakfast that was quickly eaten. Away from here— the cattle were ready to move and the men wanted to move them. No time for seconds on coffee. No time for talk. Away from here. They shook out the last drops in their cups and started toward their horses.

"One moment," said Dunson.

The drivers turned to face the bull-chested man who had sat throughout the shank of the night on the wagon tongue. Slowly he moved to his feet. His gray eyes searched among the men. At length they held on the wrangler. Dunson beckoned with a blunt forefinger.

"Step up here, Bunk Kennelly," he said. "Step up and tell why that shot was fired last night."

"The lashin' on my gun boot was worn," said Bunk.

"You've killed three men," said Dunson. "A tally will show we've lost three, four hundred steers." He reached to the seat of the cart and lifted the long bull whip Groot used on the oxen. "You'll take a dozen lashes and call yourself fortunate."

No movement by the men. No comment. But the eyes of each found those of his neighbor. Teeler Yacey drew a long breath. Dunson teased the whip through his fingers.

"Mathew, tie that man's wrists to the wheel of the cart," he said. "Help with it, Teeler."

Still no movement. Dunson swung his gray eyes toward Mathew. Challenge lived in them. A challenge that was answered. They moved to meet with Teeler's. Again there was silence while two men crossed wills. The veins in Dunson's throat pulsed red and heavy.

"Very well, then," said Dunson. "He'll take it without a wheel to rest on." And to the wrangler: "Turn around, Kennelly. Turn around or you're apt to lose an eye."

"You won't whip me," said Bunk Kennelly.

"Turn around!"

"No man whips me."

"Turn around!"

And with the words Dunson's left hand lifted the lash high. He sent it backward over his shoulder. The little wrangler's hand dropped down. His gun was half clear of the leather when there was the flat sound of a single shot. Bunk's gun clattered on the hard ground. Spun half around, the wrangler grabbed at a broken shoulder. Bewilderment was in the eyes he turned on Mathew Garth—the man who had shot him.

"Damn you, Mathew!" cried Dunson. "Why did you do that?"

"To keep him alive," said Mathew slowly. He holstered his gun that still trailed smoke. "You'd have shot him between the eyes."

"You're right!"

"That's what I figured," said Mathew. He turned away.

Dunson's stare was a dull thing as he looked at the wrangler. "Clear out, Kennelly—take your gear and ride." And to the others: "We've lost half the morning. Pick up whatever strays you can and let's get on with the drive."

The men stepped into their saddles. Cherry Valance rode beside Mathew. For a time he studied the tall man on the sorrel stud.

At length Cherry smiled and shook his head. "You're fast, Mathew," he said. "Fast—and just a little soft. That's what will kill you, some day. . . ."

The herd drove north along the Balcones fault. Brown earth gave way to red clay that lined the banks of the sandy-bottomed Colorado. Scrub oak and hackberry dotted the rolling grasslands. Good grazing for the cattle, but the men starved. They crossed Brush Creek, the Lampasas River and the narrow Leon. Long days and short nights. Tempers grew raw as flesh that is rubbed against leather.

No talk at the night fires. No laughter. Sullen men rode under a hard master. Dunson's orders were given without explanation —obeyed without question. Then a night camp on a bank of the tree-bordered Brazos when a rider drifted in out of the darkness. A shaggy man with matted hair and rags that served for clothing. He stepped down from his horse and limped to the fire. A festering wound curved in an ugly crescent across a cheek from temple to jaw. There was the mark of a rope on his neck. One boot was gone and a bloodstained sack was wrapped about the injured foot.

"Howdy," he said. And his voice was a whisper.

"Howdy," said Mathew. He flipped a slice of beef onto a tin plate and filled a cup. "Just in time to eat."

No words from the stranger until the cup was empty and the plate was clean, then: "Name is Dufrey. Was ridin' point for old man Garwood—two thousand head up from Burnet. Got 'em as far as Pine Valley in the Quachitas before the border gangs jumped us out. Killed fifteen and left me hangin'. A frayed rope kept me alive. They nailed old man Garwood's feet an' hands to a wagon wheel. Left him staked. He was dead.. when I got to him."

It was a twice-told tale in Texas. Two hundred thousand head of cattle stolen. Two hundred drivers killed. Dunson's men knew the story. Tonight it struck hard. Words are words, but this tattered remnant of a man was visual proof of what happened on the border. There was a slow shifting of boots. An equally slow exchange of glances.

Mathew stepped out of the pool of firelight and found his blanket in the wagon. He tossed it to the bearded stranger. "How many men," he asked, "were in the gang that jumped you?"

"Close to a hundred." Dufrey folded the blanket about his shoulders. "Stampeded the herd and took us as we rode out. Didn't have a chance."

"This was in the Quachitas?"

The shaggy man noded. "Too bad we didn't swing north at the Red. Heard tell of a place in Kansas where they was buildin' a railroad. Old man Garwood, he was sort of stubborn. Said maybe the railroad was there, maybe it wasn't."

"Who told you about the railroad?"

"Two, three fellers. One was Jess Chisholm, the half-breed who runs horses an' beef for the army. He told about it. Said his wagons'd marked a trail up through the Nations. Said we could follow this to the Cimarron an' maybe further."

"Who else?"

"A Kansas feller, can't think of his name. Worked for people named McCoy out of Illinois. He swore up an' down the railroad was goin' to Abilene."

Mathew turned to Dunson who stood in the half light of the fire. "Cherry saw the rails. They're past Topeka and heading west. If we swing north at the Red it's a straight drive to Kansas."

"We've started for Missouri," said Dunson slowly. "Each

of you knew what was ahead when he signed on. I'll not be turned aside by this man's story or that of anyone else."

Maler Rand shook his head. Maler Rand—a dour man from Guadalupe, back from a northern prison camp to find his home stolen by Austin politicians. A thin man with a thin throat, long dangling arms, and a cough that often left flecks of foam on his lips. A good rider, he worked the swing with Walker of Lavaca, Tom Sudden, a tall man named Kelsey and Jose Fernandez out of Matagorda. All good men—all cattlemen. And now with one accord they grouped themselves beside Maler Rand. This was the show-down.

"I've got enough," said Maler. "We're making a drive we'll never finish. I'm for Abilene or home."

Dunson walked to the cook pot. He dipped two blunt fingers into the water and lifted a slice of beef, chewing it thoroughly before he let it slide down his throat. With equal slowness he drained a cup of coffee. Then he walked to the wagon tongue that served as a throne.

"We'll finish the drive, Maler," he said. "We'll sell my steers in Missouri."

"What'll we eat on the way?"

"Beef."

"An' what'll we drink?"

"Cold water if we have to."

"Then fight a hundred men to reach the market?" Maler's laugh was short. "I've tried that kind of fightin'. It don't work. When your stomach goes, everything goes with it. That's the way the Yankees got me—too sick to fight, too weak to run."

"We'll finish the drive," said Dunson stubbornly.

"Not me," said Maler. "I'm ridin' south."

"And me," said Tom Sudden. "I got enough, unless we try for Abilene."

Kelsey nodded in agreement; so did Walker of Lavaca. Jose Fernandez of Matagorda lifted his narrow shoulders in a shrug.

"Me, I think about this thing," he said. "When we start I say, 'Jose, maybe you die. But then again, maybe you don't die, an' for three months you eat an' then you get money.' " The Mexican shook his head. "Now I know for three months I don't eat. I don't get money. I do die. So me, I go south with Maler Rand."

"Before you signed on each agreed to finish the drive," said Dunson quietly. "I mean to hold you to that agreement."

"How?" said Maler. And the word was flat.

Teeler Yacey stretched the leg that carried the saber cut; eased himself gently away from the fire. Old Leather drew a breath and moved out of line. Andres, Lovelock and Groot found things to do in the darkness. Others fanned out. Maler and his group stood their ground.

"How?" said Maler again.

Dunson's arms swung like the broken limbs of a windblown tree. The blunt fingers spread. His feet were wide, thrusting down against the earth as though they were rooted.

"I don't want to kill you, Maler," he said. "If you make me, I will."

"Like hell you will!"

As Maler spoke he went for his gun. So did Walker and Sudden and Kelsey and Jose Fernandez of Matagorda. Fast men with their guns. Deadly fast.

"*Mathew!*" said Dunson.

And even as their weapons lifted into line two guns threw death at the riders. Later, men swore Dunson's shots were an echo of Mathew's. Now it seemed the two guns blazed as one. Maler went down and Jose Fernandez grabbed at his stomach. Again the guns roared. Kelsey's shot went wild and he screamed as he lifted a hand to his face. Walker fell and Sudden nodded like a drunken man before he crumpled into a still thing on the ground. Then silence. Dark silence. Guns had spoken on the bank of the Brazos. Guns held in the hands of two master craftsmen. Cold, methodical hands that shot to kill. Now silence moved in like a night fog around the fire.

"Thank you, Mathew," said Dunson quietly. It was as though the tall rider had given him a cup of coffee.

Methodically Dunson refilled the empty chambers in his gun. As he did, he listened. So did the others—listened and waited for the first rumble of hooves that would tell them the herd had started to stampede. A steer bellowed. Another answered. Then silence again as the strange and unpredictable beasts continued to sleep.

Dunson indicated the fallen men. "Have them buried, Mathew. I'll read over them in the morning." And to the others: "We'll finish the drive to Missouri and I'll hear no more talk about Kansas."

There was no answer. Unless it was the distant rumble of thunder in the north. A Spring raindrop fell hissing into the fire. Then another. And as though it were a curtain descending upon a play rain fell over the plains of Texas.

Morning brought no letup. The stranger was given a stake from the drivers' meager store and he rode south. The herd moved north. Soft ground and washes filled with water. The land grew rougher and always less inviting. This was the Cross Timbers, a place of weirdly fantastic buttes, mad stretches of shifting sand, gorges cut by wind and water. There was mesquite and low cactus that suddenly gave way to dense growths of scrub oak. And still it rained.

The drive swung west toward higher ground and the men shivered in their saddles. They nooned wherever there was shelter from the wind and Groot brewed coffee that was little better than the water that dripped from the wide hat brims. But it was hot. The long-haired cook was a wizard at fire building and somehow managed to keep a constant supply of dry wood in the hide cady nailed to the bottom of the wagon.

Rain through the night. It slipped in under the folds of Mathew's tarp. It squeezed into his boots and filled them to overflowing as he rode guard. The cattle were standing; too wet to bed down, the long-horned beasts gathered in bunches and bawled their protests to the teeming heavens. Mathew watched a reluctant dawn creep over the eastern edge of the earth.

He checked the remuda. Three horses were gone. With them

had gone Reed Atchison, Baldy McLean and Will Sutter. Good men, these. Good men but they'd had enough. Rather than fight, they'd simply slipped away in the darkness. Mathew reported the loss to Dunson.

"Groot!" called the huge man. "Look in the wagon and see if we're short."

"Did look," said Groot. "Lost a sack of flour an' beans. Lost a hunnerd cartridges. Lost a small sack of salt an' coffee."

Dunson turned to Cherry Valance who stood near the fire. "Take Teeler Yacey and three others. Bring those men back!"

"They may object," said Cherry quietly.

"Bring them back!" Dunson turned and motioned to Mathew. "Start the drive."

For a long moment Mathew looked at Cherry Valance. The dark man caught the look and when Mathew stepped into his saddle Cherry reined his horse alongside that of the segundo.

"Worried?"

"A little."

"I'll be back," said Cherry. "When it comes time for me to quit I'll step up like Maler did."

Cherry's words built a picture. A dark, mad-eyed, laughing man with murder in his mind and a gun in his hand. The fastest gun in Texas, so they said. A gun that had killed twenty men. "It won't be nice," said Mathew. "It won't be nice when you step up to Dunson."

"You'll stand with him again?"

"Yes."

"Why?"

"We made an agreement."

"Dunson isn't using common sense," said Cherry. "We'll never get through to Missouri. You know that, Mathew."

"It's Dunson's herd."

"It's your life," said Cherry. He motioned to Teeler and turned once more to grin at Mathew. "And every day they're building that railroad closer to Abilene...."

Mathew turned his stud toward the herd as Cherry and his

men rode south. He teased out the lead steer and built his point. There was trail now. Trail left by other herds that had started for Missouri. It snaked north across the Trinity, growing ever more definite as it reached toward the northern boundary of Texas. The herd followed its pattern. Weary riders urged the sullen cattle along. Drive all day. Sleep wet at night. And always and ever there was Thomas Dunson at their heels.

Then a day when they reached the Red River. The herd was held a mile from the bank while Mathew rode forward with Dunson. Rain had done its work and the Red was up. White water in the narrows, bubbling, frothing, churning water that raced along between caving banks that melted away even as the two men watched. Twisting trunks of mighty trees tumbled in mad confusion. Fountains that jetted high above boulders that once marked the limits of the ford. The Red was up.

Above the narrows the river spilled across a mile of flatlands. A moment while Dunson considered, then he rode deliberately into the brown flood. Mathew followed. Sand spewed up in churning bubbles that dragged at the horses' legs. An eighth of a mile and the bottom fell away abruptly. Mathew slipped from the saddle to ease his stud, holding to a leather tie. Dunson did likewise. The horses swam a hundred yards before they floundered onto a sandbar.

"We'd do better to wait," said Mathew. "The rain's stopped and the river will be down in a few days."

For answer Dunson urged his mount forward. Soon both horses were drifting downstream as they fought against the drag of the river. Somehow they made the far bank. Somehow they recrossed the river. It lacked an hour of sunset and the wind had an edge. Cold closed like a blanket about Mathew and he fought the chill in his legs while Dunson studied the crossing.

"I don't want the sun in their eyes when they're swimming," said Dunson finally. "As soon as it's down we'll put them in."

"They'll like it better in the morning."

"We'll cross tonight."

"I figure," said Mathew quietly, "you've got a reason to make tired men work a herd through cold water at night."

"I have," said Dunson.

"For a lot of years," said Mathew, as the horses started back toward camp, "I've taken your orders without any questions. You're the boss. I'm your segundo. But sometimes a man begins to wonder."

"Yes, Mathew," said Dunson slowly. "Sometimes a man begins to wonder. He wonders what will happen to the things he's built. Wonders how long they'll last after he's gone."

"What things?"

Dunson lifted his hands and looked at the blunt fingers that grew from two calloused palms. "The things he's made with his own two hands—the house and barns he's built, the stables and corrals. I've built these things, Mathew. I've built an empire! It's mine! These hands made it out of nothing . . . !" One heavy arm swung toward the herd bunched on the bed grounds. "I've built it—and now I must find a market for my beef or the whole thing crumbles into nothing." His voice grew an edge. "Some nights ago we lost three men. I haven't slept since and we haven't lost any more. We won't lose any tonight, nor tomorrow!"

"How will you hold them?" asked Mathew.

"With weariness," said Dunson. "I'll keep this herd moving until Cherry and his men get back. Then, by God, we'll see if there are any others who want to ride south!" He turned those hard gray eyes on Mathew. "Does that answer your question?"

"Sort of," said Mathew. He rode to the fire and motioned to the grouped riders. "Start them along. We'll cross tonight."

A moment while the men let the words tell their story. A moment while thirteen tired riders glanced toward the herd, then back toward the tall man on the sorrel stud. A night crossing? Cold water and a sullen herd, riders worn to exhaustion, half a night in the saddle with a black wind cutting through wet clothes—why?

"You'll put 'em in cold?" said Laredo Downs. Silent, usually, the dark rider shook his head. "Every steer in that herd'll start thinkin' of home. It can't be done."

"We'll do it," said Mathew. "Start them along."

He turned his stud toward the herd and teased out the lead steer. The monstrous beast lifted its head. The needle-tipped horns swung in a vicious thrust that missed Mathew's leg by a scant few inches. Laredo Downs rode in to help. "Hi-yaaa!" And the riatas swirled and slashed. "Hi-yaaa! Git along, git along . . . !" Protest in the herd. A bawling, deep-throated protest that lifted in a crescendo of sound. "Hi-yaaa! Git along . . . !"

The horses wheeled and leaped clear of the swinging horns. Mathew and Laredo built their point. The swing men hustled the others along. Soon the herd was moving. Riders in the drag urged them at a faster pace. A quarter mile, a half mile; faster and faster. When the leaders reached the river they were moving at a shuffling run. Dunson marked the spot on the low bank. The drivers ran the herd toward it.

A two-foot drop and below it knee-deep brown water. Mathew jumped his stud into the river. The lead steer hit the bank and went over. Then another. "Hi-yaaa! Git along, steer!" The men popped their quirts and shouted, pushing the cattle almost on top of those in the water. A dozen beeves balked at the bank but the pressure of those coming up from behind sent them on.

"Put them in!" called Dunson. "Crowd them—get the herd in before they start swimming!"

In the wild muddy waters dotted with floating tree trunks over two thousand steers had hit the first deep section and were swimming toward the middle of the stream. Mathew and the riders in the water swam their horses along the lower flanks, fighting to keep the animals headed upstream. Still Dunson and his men sent them in.

Then it happened. This thing—this terror that haunted the river crossings whenever a drive was made. The longhorns began to mill. Caught by the current and swept past the line of swimming horses, the steers lost direction. Within a moment the full two thousand were a mad, senseless whirlpool of tossing horns. Reason was gone. So, too, was any instinct for self-preservation. Around and around like some monstrous top, they spun in a great circle in the muddy waters.

"Into them!" cried Mathew. "Move into them!"

No need for the order. Laredo and the drivers swam their courageous little mounts hard into the swirling mass. One job to do. Only one. Break this mad maelstrom and send the steers toward one bank or the other. Forget the crossing. Forget everything but the task at hand. The riders yelled. They fired their guns. They lashed at the faces of the swimming cattle.

There was a break in the mass. Mathew's stud had forced a group downstream. Horse and rider turned them back toward the south bank. Back toward the ford where Dunson and the remaining riders were now fighting to hold the confused remainder of the herd. Others followed. Swimming blindly and stupidly they reached shallow water and splashed toward a break in the bank. A lunging leap put the lead steer on firm ground. Riders hazed him away from the river. Others, working in the muddy water, kept the line moving. Within an hour the herd was once again bunched on the same bed ground —the herd, all but a hundred odd that now floated south and east on the flood waters of the Red.

Faithful Groot kept his fire blazing high near a stand of oaks a half mile distant from the herd. Hard beef and sour coffee. Then the sound of a high, echoing cry in the night. Too tired to stand, the drivers watched listlessly as a strange procession rode to the fire. Cherry Valance and Teeler Yacey, and with them were six men. Two riders sat with their wrists lashed to the saddle horns. The others dismounted and walked to the coffee boiler.

Dunson waited until Cherry Valance had emptied his cup. "I sent you after three men."

"Baldy McLean figured he'd rather fight," said Cherry. "Made a good fight. Took Oscar Tellman along with him. We buried them both."

Dunson nodded toward the prisoners. "Bring them to the wagon."

The big man took his place on the wagon tongue. Atchison and Sutter stood before him, their hands still bound. Silence dropped over the camp. Above was the Texas moon—round, hard, utterly cold. It looked down on the grouped men. In the outer darkness a steer bawled. A horse stamped impatiently. And far off in the night there was the weird, hacking cry of the coyote.

"Reed Atchison and William Sutter," said Dunson, "you took employment with me and agreed to certain conditions. Is that so?"

"We did," said Atchison.

"You agreed to finish the drive to Missouri."

"That's right," said Atchison. "But we changed our minds."

"You stole flour, coffee, beans and salt," said Dunson. "You stole three horses and killed Oscar Tellman."

"Baldy killed Oscar," said Sutter. "It was a fair fight."

"Fair . . . ?" said Dunson. And the word was a curse. "What would you know about fairness?" He pointed toward the sleeping cattle. "Every dollar I own is in that herd—every hour I've lived! You knew it when you signed on. You knew it when you stole flour and beans and coffee and salt from the wagon. You're a thief, Sutter!"

"The law might think different."

"*I'm* the law," said Dunson. "And I say you're a thief. You, too, Atchison." He turned to Mathew, motioned with that blunt thumb toward the clump of near-by trees. "Hang them both."

It wasn't unexpected. From the moment he talked with Dunson at the river Mathew had known what the ultimate must be. Perhaps Dunson was right. Perhaps it was the only way to hold the drive together. But the words were sudden, harsh.

Mathew looked at Atchison—looked at Sutter. Both were young. Both wanted to live.

"It might be," said Mathew slowly, "they'd promise to finish the drive. I'd take their word."

"Hang them!"

No argument; only these two words. Mathew looked toward the half circle of silent riders. Each man turned away. Each man—until Mathew came to a pair of eyes that held twin devils. Cherry Valance rested an elbow on his saddle and stared back. Mathew pointed to the coiled riata. "If you'll drop that over Atchison's neck," he said evenly, "there's a low limb on that far oak."

"It's a good riata," said Cherry. "I wouldn't want to lose it."

"Five minutes' stretching won't hurt it."

Mathew cast off the lashings of his own and dropped the noose over Sutter's head. A smile tugged at the corners of Cherry's mouth as he snapped the braided loop in a quick cast about Atchison's neck. The prisoners were mounted and led to the oak; their wrists were lashed to their belts. Cherry coiled the ends of both riatas and looked up to judge the height of the limb. As he did, Mathew reined close to Atchison.

"Ride, you fool!" he whispered. "You can't win, but ride!"

With the words the bound man jabbed his spurred heels against the flanks of his mount. Sutter did the same. Both mustangs leaped forward. The riatas were whipped from Cherry's hand as the men headed downstream. Cherry's gun was out. So was Mathew's. Both were slow. Seconds slow. But not Dunson. There was a splash of flame near the wagon tongue. Then another. Two hard, flat echoes danced over the Texas plain. And two riderless horses ran wild.

"Catch those horses!" said Dunson. He holstered his gun.

The group near the wagon broke. Tense men suddenly released from tension, they spun their horses in hasty pursuit. Away from the wagon. Away from the two things that lay on the red earth. And under the oak tree a dark, cynical rider looked into a pair of dull gray eyes.

"I heard what you said to Atchison," said Cherry.
"Did you?"

Cherry nodded. "You're fast with your head as well as your gun. But just a little soft, Mathew. . . ."

In the early morning Dunson read over two flat graves. A short reading because there was the Red River to cross before the sun came up. He closed the Bible, stored it carefully in the wagon and rode toward the bed grounds at the head of a sullen group of riders. The steers were on the prod, mean, asking for trouble. Cherry eyed them thoughtfully as he rode in to build point.

"Met a man while we were bringing in Sutter and Atchison," he said casually. "He was just down from the Llano Estacado, and he claims there's a good crossing above Mud Creek."

"Where's that?" asked Dunson.

"A hundred miles west of here."

"West?" Dunson shook his head. "Eight days going—another eight driving back on the far side. Forget it. We'll cross here."

"Might be we wouldn't drive back," said Mathew as he stepped his stud forward. "If we cross at Mud Creek we can swing north through the Nations. That's buffalo country—good grass. Good grass all the way to Kansas, and a railroad waiting when we get there."

Teeler Yacey rubbed his aching hip. "Sounds good to me."

"Me, too," said Old Leather Monte.

"I'm for swingin' west," said Kemper Vale, a lean man with high, knoblike cheekbones and a black beard. "Might mean another week or two on the trail—might be a month. Might meet a few Indians in the Nations, but I'll take them against the border crowd."

"Me, too," said Laredo Downs. "I favor goin' west."

Others nodded in agreement. Some added a word in support of Mathew's plan. Dunson waited until the last rider had had his say. Slowly, ponderously, he straightened himself in his saddle.

"So you've heard of a railroad that's building to Kansas...."
His laugh was a dull thing, heavy with ridicule. "I've heard of others they were going to build—one that was supposed to go all the way to California. A nice dream. But only a dream. Just like your railroad to Kansas." He turned to face Cherry Valance. "What's the name of this town where you expect to find a stockyard?

"Abilene."

"Ever been there?"

"No."

"I've been to Missouri," said Dunson. "I saw cows bring fifteen, eighteen, twenty dollars at the yard. The buyers paid cash and asked for more beef. We'll drive to Missouri."

"Where do you mean to cross the Red?" asked Mathew.

"Here."

"You figure to lose a few head?"

"A thousand if I must," said Dunson.

"How many men?"

Dunson's heavy hand swung dangerously close to his gun. "Talk, talk and be damned to your talk, Mathew!" He backed his horse and faced the group. "I've heard enough! *Drive, damn you, or go for your guns!*"

For a long moment they looked silently at the man. Dunson would fight. He'd kill or be killed. One after another they turned away. And once again the herd was driven toward the river. Once again Mathew sent his sorrel leaping from the low bank into the muddy water. Ropes whirled and riders shouted. The herd followed like an avalanche, spilling over the bank and struggling madly across the shallows. They reached the section where the sweeping waters had gouged out a space of river bed. They swam, stumbled onto hard ground and were again forced into deep water by the mass that followed.

Slowly the natural leaders forged ahead, following the sorrel stud that was swimming hard for the distant bank. Here was a horse! A gallant sire of a breed destined to leave its mark upon the entire West. A Quarter Horse—born with a job to do; born to work cattle. Wide-eyed and wise, Mathew broke him at three, worked him at four, called him Old Billy and made him his stud. Now they were partners, fighting the drag of the river, herding the swimming cattle in a long reach across the current.

The line bent slowly, swinging in a wide U that reached out toward the far bank. A hundred yards, two hundred. Suddenly the stud's feet struck solid ground. There was a break in the bank and Mathew put him up it. The lead steer followed. Then another. Soon a dozen dripping beasts stumbled onto the grassy plain and looked stupidly about.

Mathew rode back toward the river. The curve was deepening, easing downstream. Two swing men, Barney Saul and Grant Shallert, swam their horses at the low bend of the U. Busy with the work, they failed to see destruction coming toward them. It moved swiftly—a half-submerged tree trunk that disappeared at times then leaped high as it struck against a rock.

"Break the line!" cried Mathew. "Barney—let that tree through!"

Too late the rider tried to turn a swimming steer. Too late the animal saw the tree trunk whirling toward it. The wide horns took the thrust. Driven backward the steer crashed into the next in line. Lunging, struggling to climb up and over the twisting trunk a third steer was caught. Then another. Barney's horse tried to fight clear of the mass. A longhorn swept the rider from the saddle. A single cry. Then rider and horse were caught.

Mathew threw his stud down the bank. Swam him parallel to the oncoming steers. Cherry was there, a shouting, cursing man who urged his own mount through the water. The U was broken. Twisted backward at the base and easing off downstream in a snakelike line. Panic caught the leaders and they started to mill. Shallert tried to break the mass. He was hooked by a horn and whirled into maelstrom. Cherry Valance moved in toward the slashing hooves and horns.

"Let them go!" called Mathew. "Cherry—let them go and break the line!"

It was the only way. On the far bank Dunson motioned to the near-by riders and sent his horse into the water. The huge man swam his mount hard at the line, trying to head the beasts that had not yet reached the spinning mass. Teeler joined him. So did Kavanaugh and Nambel. No time for Barney Saul. No time for Grant Shallert. They were gone but that line *must* be turned. And the riders fought like madmen.

The drag of the river fought against them. It pulled the swimming animals downstream where a steer stumbled onto footing that suddenly gave way beneath its weight. An island in the stream—but an island of quicksand. A second steer crowded close upon the first. Then a third and a fourth. Plunging, bellowing animals that mired themselves deeper with each forward step. Slowly the spotted carpet of hides spread. A hundred steers belly deep and going deeper.

"Stop them at the bank!" called Mathew. He motioned to the men sending the cattle into the river. "Stop them at the bank!"

"Keep them coming!" yelled Dunson. And then to Mathew: "I'll give the orders, Mathew!"

"You're mad! You'll lose them all!"

*"Keep them coming!"* bellowed Dunson to the men on the bank. *"Keep those steers coming!"*

He sent his horse at the nearest animal. Unmindful of the needle-tipped horn that ripped through his jacket. Unmindful of the torn flesh beneath it. Bellowing now, raging at the beasts—more like a great bull than a man. His heavy fists flailed at the steers' heads, hammered against their snouts, fought to turn them upstream.

Suddenly Dunson split the line. Turned it with an insane fury nothing could stand against. A new U formed. The raging man goaded the lead steer upstream, beating at the beast's head. Other steers followed. The riders strung out along the under side of the new U and sent the cattle on toward ground that would hold under their feet.

Sims Reeves tried to help. Little Sims Reeves who worked in the drag. But Sims couldn't swim and his horse was done. Forced to carry the entire weight of its rider, the brown head slipped beneath the surface. Coughing, blinded, crazed, the horse turned and struck out downstream. There were steers ahead, mired deep.

"Turn him!" cried Mathew. "Reeves—turn him, you fool!"

It was too late. Already the horse was wallowing in the treacherous sand. A steer's horn crossed its neck. An instant of struggle. Then steer and horse and rider were down, threshing in the soft sands of the trap. Long horns tossed above them. Mad beasts lunged this way and that. And on the far bank Old Leather Monte, boss of the drag, saw his rider's danger.

"Reeves!" he called. "Reeves, boy—lift an arm!"

Old Leather rode his horse shoulder deep into the brown water. He spun his riata in a true cast toward the arm that reached upward. Almost the grasping fingers caught the loop. Almost, then a steer swung its head and the arm went down. Old Leather closed his eyes as he hauled in the riata and coiled it slowly. For a moment he sat his horse in the muddy water. Then a cry came from the far bank.

"Monte! Keep them coming!" It was Dunson's voice. *"Keep those steers coming!"*

Dunson had rebuilt the U; looped it across the river. Steers were climbing onto dry ground. Onto the grasslands beyond. He'd started a line of heaving broad backs that moved throughout the morning. A line that broke occasionally when flotsam of the river drove a struggling group downstream to join those already buried in the quicksand. Hour upon hour the line moved on. The wagon crossed, lashed to tree trunks. And Groot built his inevitable fire on the far bank.

At times a rider would hurry to the fire, snatch a hasty slab of beef and a scalding swallow of coffee. Then back into the water. A thousand head on the far bank; two thousand; riders that rolled in their saddles and fell when they tried to dismount.

"Keep those steers coming!" Dunson's voice goaded them on. A Dunson who never rested, never stopped. And at last the herd stood bunched on the far side of the Red River.

The next day was spent in camp. The cattle grazed. The men let life creep back into their tortured bodies. Too tired to talk, too tired to think, they huddled near the fire. At noon Dunson roused himself to sit silently on the wagon tongue. When the sun reached toward the far horizon he wakened the men and walked ahead of them to the river bank. Silently, he stood beside the acre of death. He opened the soiled pages of the Bible.

"I'll read for Grant Shallert, for Barney Saul, for Sims Reeves," he said. "Take off your hats."

The riders uncovered and the strange man read. Read the lines that tell us: "I am the resurrection and the life. . . ." Read while the beef steers bawled and the horses stamped in protest against the flies that swarmed about their legs. While Mathew looked at the place where three men had died, then at the riders left of the original thirty. Thirteen men. Thirteen sons of Texas who stood quietly while Dunson continued: "Man that is born of woman, hath but a short time to live, and is full of misery. . . ." Then the Bible snapped shut.

"Rest tonight," said Dunson. "Tomorrow we'll start for Missouri."

"No," said Mathew. He put on his wide-brimmed hat. "I won't drive to Missouri. Thirteen men can't fight the border gangs."

Once again the huge man leveled his eyes at those of his segundo. Gray on gray—challenge and answer. And this time there was no turning away. Mathew's head was high, higher than Dunson's. His feet were wide spread. His arms swung loose. Almost it was as though he were an image of the older man—an image that had grown taller and straighter and equally strong.

"I won't drive to Missouri," he said again.

Dunson's voice was soft. "Do we drive without you, Mathew?"

"You do."

Now Teeler stepped forward. "And without me."

"And me," said Lovelock. "I've had enough."

One after another the men stepped forward to stand beside Mathew. Some added a comment. Most stepped forward in silence. Andres and Kinney and Laredo Downs, Evans and Kavanaugh, Joe Nambel and Slim Dale—Dunson looked hard at each.

He turned to Old Leather. "And you, too, Monte?"

Monte shook his head. "I made an agreement. I'll keep it."

"What about you, Jargens?"

"I'll keep the word I gave."

"So will I," said Brick Keever.

Dunson glanced at Cherry Valance. The dark curls caught the last glints of the setting sun as Cherry shook his head. "I'm for Kansas."

"That leaves you three riders," said Mathew. "They're not enough, Dunson."

"Get out!" Dunson's gaze washed over Mathew like a wave of flame. "I'll finish the drive without you. Finish it with these three and whatever men I can pick up along the way."

"Even you can't do that."

"I can try, damn you!"

"You can't try because I won't let you," said Mathew. "I'm taking this herd to Kansas."

For a moment the men of the drive forgot to breathe. They forgot the river, the herd, the great plains that stretched northward across the Indian Nations. Two men held the stage. Two men whose hands swung loosely above their guns. Two men whose eyes were on fire.

"You're taking my herd?" said Dunson slowly. "You're taking *my* herd to Kansas?"

"I don't figure it's your herd," said Mathew. "Not yours alone. It's something that belongs to Texas—to every cattleman who's starving at home while a market waits in the north. You taught me this, Dunson—taught me others will follow if we show the way. That's big. Bigger than me. Bigger than you. It's big as all of Texas."

"That's *my* herd." Dunson's words fell like stones that are dropped into a deep well. "That's *my* herd."

Mathew's head moved slowly. "The money is yours. I'll leave it on deposit in Kansas, less only the pay that goes to the riders. This herd belongs to the people of Texas. I mean to drive it to market."

"Mathew," said Dunson. "I'm going to kill you."

"And when you do," said Mathew, "will you kill Cherry and Laredo and Slim and Nambel? Will you kill Andres and Teeler and the rest?"

"I'm going to kill you," whispered Dunson.

The fingers spread on the heavy right hand. But as it moved a shot hammered against the stillness. Not from Mathew's gun, although it was clear of its holster. Rather, the bullet that tore muscle and flesh from Dunson's shoulder came from the gun held in Cherry's hand. A gun that had been quietly drawn while the men talked. One that was now lined on Mathew's chest to stop the sweep of the tall man's weapon toward Cherry Valance—to stop the hammer that was being thumbed into place.

"Only a shoulder, Mathew," said Cherry. Laughter was in the eyes that looked over the gun barrel. "The same as you did for the wrangler. I'd call it a favor to you both."

"I do my own shooting."

"You might have been slow," said Cherry. He moved with a catlike step. His left hand picked up Dunson's gun and kicked out the shells. He dropped the empty weapon back into the worn leather below Dunson's hip. "Yes, Mathew, you might have been slow and I don't want to go to Missouri."

Mathew motioned to the cook. "Groot—see what you can do for that shoulder."

"Never mind the shoulder," said Dunson. He stood erect,

both arms dangling while blood oozed through the torn flesh and dripped from his fingertips.

"Have it your way," said Mathew. Again he motioned to Groot. "Flour, coffee, beans and salt—fifty cartridges and whatever else you can spare. Put it in a sack and lash it to Dunson's saddle." Mathew gestured to Laredo. "Cut his horse out of the remuda."

"You're turning me loose?" asked Dunson.

"I am."

"That's a mistake, Mathew." Dunson's voice was low, held in control by that iron will. "You're a thief, now. You and your men. I'll spread your names across the face of Texas. Thieves and outlaws—there'll be no room on the range for any of you. Remember that."

"I'll try to remember," said Mathew.

The men stood quietly while Laredo roped Dunson's horse and tossed the saddle into place. The sack was made fast and above it was lashed Dunson's tarp and blanket. There was no move by Dunson. No word.

"Good-bye," said Mathew dully. "The money will be in Abilene."

The huge man stepped into his saddle, trailing an arm that spread a red stain across the horse's rump. He turned to look down at Mathew Garth. "You've stolen my herd," he said. "But you'll never drive it to market. Not to Abilene nor anywhere else. I'll come back, Mathew. I'll find a dozen men in Texas to ride with me—a dozen men who think as I do about thieves and outlaws. I'll find you, Mathew. And when I do I'll hang you and your men to the nearest tree!"

Fury gripped him—rage that swelled the veins of the huge man's throat. It purpled his cheeks and drew a dull film over his eyes. Somehow he lifted the injured arm. Somehow he doubled the fingers into a clublike bloodstained fist—reached it upward as though to call down the vengeance of the heavens upon this man who had stolen his beef.

"Mathew Garth!" he cried. "Damn the day I found you!

Damn the mother that bred you! I'll be back, Mathew! I'll be back to see you hang!"

A great hand wrenched the horse's head about. Spurred heels dug deeply into the beast's flanks. A leap that covered twenty feet and the horse raced madly toward the river bank. No pause. The wide chest hit the stream and the horse struck out for the far side. Mathew stood motionless. So did the others. Motionless and just a little awed by the savage intensity of Dunson's words. Suddenly there was a laugh that lifted through four notes of the octave as Cherry turned to walk back to the fire. Others followed. Mathew stood alone, looking south across the foaming river toward Texas. . . .

The herd moved north. North and west into the unknown. Texas was behind them. These were the "Nations"—land held for untold centuries by the Indians. Land which later would be called the State of Oklahoma, but which now was a battleground. Wide, sweeping plains, rivers in flood, the Washita, Canadian, the Cimarron and the Arkansas—and between these rivers were tribes of sullen red men, goaded from their lands by the westward swing of the whites. Choctaws, Chickasaws, Cherokees and Osages, Kiowas, Creeks, Apaches and Comanches—restless, angry, eager for trouble. And to the east, a more dangerous brood—the white savages of the Arkansas and Missouri borders.

North and west, along the faint outlines of the Chisholm Trail to the Cherokee Strip where the first giant herds of buffalo darkened the horizon. Mathew rode point with Cherry Valance. A silent, thoughtful Mathew who studied the ears of his sorrel stud while over and again the words of Thomas Dunson came back to plague him. *"You've stolen my herd—you'll never drive it to market . . ."* Over and again the hooves of his stud drummed it up from the earth: *"You've stolen my herd! . . . stolen my herd! . . . stolen my herd!"*

"You think he'll come back?" said Cherry quietly. It was as though the man could read the thoughts that lived in Mathew's mind.

"He'll come back."

"It's a long road."

"He'll come back."

A moment while Cherry rode silently. Then he lifted an arm to point toward a distant rider. Teeler Yacey, sent ahead to scout the land and mark the line of the next day's drive. The tall man was sending his horse along at a pace that drew both riders erect in their saddles. Trouble—a river in flood, stampeding buffalo, Indians, any one of a thousand things, but they all added up to trouble. Mathew and Cherry rode out to meet the man on the foam-covered horse.

"*Coffee!*" he yelled. "I had *coffee!* I had biscuits an' beans an' sowbelly an' *pie!*"

Cherry looked wisely at Mathew. "Crazy as hell."

"I ain't crazy!" said Teeler. He pointed a long arm toward the northern horizon. "Met a wagon train. One like you never saw in your born days. Women in it—fancy girls with pretty faces!" The words tumbled over themselves as Teeler gestured again to the north. "Two whole wagons full of women..."

"Never mind about the women," said Mathew. "Will they trade us coffee for beef?"

"Never mind about the coffee!" laughed Cherry. "Tell us more about the women!"

Lovelock and Laredo rode forward from the swing. Others joined them, caught by the excited gestures of the otherwise taciturn Teeler Yacey. Each put in a word. Each asked a question. And bit by bit the story was told: A six-wagon group, moving west—as strange a wagon train as ever crossed the plains. Clark Donegal, gambler and saloon keeper, known along both banks of the Mississippi from New Orleans to St. Louis—Clark Donegal was moving west!

Caught by the tales of new gold that had been found in Nevada, *the* Clark Donegal had loaded his bar and his wheels, his card tables and dice games, chairs and whiskey, glasses and mirrors, women and fiddle players—loaded them all into six Conestoga wagons and headed west for Nevada! At the moment the train was a day's drive north and east of the herd!

"An' they got coffee!" cried Teeler. "Coffee what tastes *just like coffee!*"

"It must be all of two months since I've had any—coffee," said Cherry. The mad lights whirled in his dark eyes as he turned to Mathew. "Why are we waiting?" He spun his horse.

"Hold it, Cherry! You, too, Laredo—all of you men!" Mathew lifted a hand. His eyes held the glaze of gray bullets in a pistol cylinder, reminiscent to the men who faced him. "The wagon train is a day to the north. We'll keep driving. Tomorrow night you'll all have coffee. Not before."

There was a murmur of disappointment. A challenging grin from Cherry. Then Laredo nodded and rode back to the swing. The drag men followed. Others grouped about Teeler for a last question—another thin shred of information. Was it *real* coffee . . . ? Real pie with apples in it . . . ? Real *women* . . . ?

*"Hi-yaaa! Git along steers! Git along!"* And the drive moved on. Faster now. Laughing men rode the swing. Laughing men urged the drag to greater speed. Never mind the dust. Never mind the bellows of anger from the herd. *"Hi-yaaa! Git along!"* Cherry strung out the lead steers, teased out the point. At times he turned to ride beside the silent Mathew. At times he chuckled. *"Git along . . . !"*

At sunset the herd slowed. Grazing time, and the great beasts tried to follow the lessons they'd learned on the drive. The riders laughed. "Hi-yaaa! Git along . . . !" Another mile. Just one more. Another mile closer to coffee and sowbelly. The men played with the words at the camp fire, chewed hard beef and pretended they were already eating soft, fluffy biscuits. They smacked their lips over scalding brown water and rolled into their blankets to dream of pie and butter and other things that haunt a man on the long drive to Kansas.

Daybreak found them well on the trail. Two miles, four— the lead steers bawled in mournful protest at the pace set by the pointers. Six miles, eight—and as the tip of the drive swung over a low hill, the great beasts lifted their heads. Water! A cool stream that flowed between tree-lined banks. And beside the stream were wagons.

Mathew rode out a little from the herd. Three miles distant six Conestogas were drawn into a tight circle. Good practice in Indian country. The fires were built within the ring and the stock held there in safety. There was movement beside the wagons. Figures that ran out a few yards and stood in groups. Then mounted men spurred their horses toward the great herd that wound over the hill.

"Keep them moving!" called Mathew. "The steers don't know wagons. They're on their muscle. We'll cross and bed on the far side."

Cherry sat his horse beside Mathew as the first of the wagon group rode up. A dark man dressed in leather, long hair brushed the shoulders of his jacket and moccasins curled about the narrow rings of his stirrups. Tom Jessup—scout and Indian fighter who for a fee would undertake to guide a wagon train across a continent.

"Howdy." He measured Mathew and Cherry with a single glance. "Your man says you're up from Texas. Meet any Indians in the Nations?"

"Saw a few smokes," said Mathew. "Saw some sign. Didn't see any Indians."

"You're lucky. Griswold an' his cavalry have got 'em on the prod, tryin' to move 'em off their ground. They mean trouble." Jessup looked back over the herd that reached toward the horizon. "You're drivin' to Kansas?"

"Abilene," said Mathew. "Ever hear of it?"

"Been there a few times."

"Did you ever hear tell of a railroad going there?"

"Never did," said Jessup, after thought. He gestured toward four men who had followed him. "Don Everman, Tod Ferris, Seven Phillips an' Cloney Crater—work for the Donegal. You'll meet him when you get to the wagons." Again he looked at the herd. "We been eatin' buffalo a lot. Could use some beef. Might be you'd trade beef for coffee?"

"Might be," said Mathew. "But you never heard about a railroad?"

"Not to Abilene—never did."

Mathew glanced at Donegal's men. They were hard—hard in a vastly different manner from the trail drivers. Theirs were the eyes of the great vultures that sweep down from the skies to prey on dead things. Each man wore gloves. Each wore a gun. Each sat his horse silently, studying the cattle and the men who drove them as the herd moved past.

"Keep them moving!" Mathew called to his men.

The lead steers rumbled heavily down the slope toward the stream. Held in line by the swing men, urged along by the pressure of the drag. Mathew eased the point away from the wagons. As they drew nearer he heard a woman laugh. Saw her wave a hand to the riders. Others in the group called out. The riders waved in reply.

"Keep them moving!" called Mathew.

Joe Nambel raked a sudden spur along the flank of his mustang. The horse gave equally sudden answer—broke in half, head between its knees, bucking, leaping, spinning.

"Hi-yaaa!" cried Nambel. "Dance for the ladies! Hi-yaaa!"

Shrill feminine cries answered: "Ride 'im! Ride 'im! Ride 'im pretty!" The women waved and laughed. Andres and Lovelock bucked their mounts. More laughter came from the wagons. And steadily, slowly, the herd drifted down toward the stream, kept in movement by the orders of the tall cold man who rode point.

Again Mathew looked toward the wagons. A dozen women, perhaps more. Women who even in the reaches of the Cherokee Strip had painted their lips and darkened their lashes. Brittle faces. Eyes that were filled with the mockery of men. Coarse laughter and equally coarse words. They called to Mathew and one swayed her hips.

A man came from the ring to join them—a heavy-shouldered man with a flaming red beard. He stood, looking off toward the herd. One of the women rested a hand on his shoulder.

He brushed her aside as though she were an insect. The Donegal's hand was rough.

"Keep them moving!" called Mathew.

It was then another woman came to stand beside the red giant. Different from the others. Even at this distance Mathew knew her. Knew her instantly as the woman who had sung at the *River Palace* in Memphis. He tried not to stare. Tried to look away. For a moment he succeeded. Then his eyes were drawn slowly back to the woman who watched him.

Hers was a white face, untouched by the sun or the scorching wind. White, save for the thin lines of her lips. Her hair was the color of grain that bends before the blade of the reaper. Thin brows, dark as the lashes beneath them. But all of this woman lived in her eyes. Strange, probing pools that held the liquid flames of twin emeralds. They met with Mathew's—calm, dispassionate, and terribly cold. The eyes of Tess Millay.

Mathew's hand went to the brim of his hat. He lifted it. Again, strangely, he heard the words she'd used that night in Memphis: *"I know we'll meet again, Mathew!"* Would she remember? Did she know him? She gave no sign. Silently, and with no change of expression she watched Mathew ride past. And beside her the red giant watched in equal silence.

"Beautiful, isn't she?" said Cherry.

"Very beautiful."

"Do you like her?"

"I wouldn't know."

Cherry's laugh had an edge. "That's where we differ, Mathew. I know what I like. Usually I find ways to get it."

Just this, but Mathew Garth knew trouble had come to the drive. Trouble that wore a fair skin and a golden crown, but trouble, nevertheless. . . .

# 5

NIGHT reached in from the east and the herd was bedded down on the far side of the stream. There was action at the water's edge—furious action as the men rubbed and scrubbed at the dirt that covered their bodies. A sharp-bladed knife, a dab of water, and Lovelock cursed as he scraped at the beard on his cheeks. His long hair was cut square at the forehead and again at the nape of his neck, parted with his fingers and slicked down hard. Women at the wagons! Fancy women with painted lips!

The riders had drawn lots for the first night guard and the mournful voices of the unlucky pair drifted in from the rim of the herd. The fire burned low, untended and forgotten. No need of a fire tonight. No need to gulp the scalding brew Groot had made in the boiler. Supper at the wagons! Clark Donegal had sent his invitation to the riders. Sent it along with two bottles of whiskey. Fiery stuff that set young Buster McGee to coughing and choking when it came his turn to tilt a bottle to his lips.

"Here, boy," said Groot and reached for the bottle. "Didn' no one tell you whiskey was for men?" He rattled the liquid around in his mouth then swallowed it in a gulp. "Store whiskey! An' t'night I eat vittles cooked by someone else than me!"

"Cooked by a woman," said Buster.

" 'Taint so!" said Groot, outraged. *"Ain't no woman can cook.* They got a black man at the fire—saw him myself."

There was laughter from the men. Then Mathew ran his fingers through his wet hair and put on his hat. "About the whiskey," he said quietly. "Not that I hold it against a man getting drunk, but we don't want fights."

"Fights . . . ?" laughed Groot. "No man can fight with me tonight. I love everybody! I love the whole world!" He twisted the ends of his long black mustache. "Most especially that little fat girl with the black hair an' red lips!"

Again there was laughter—laughter that was echoed in a higher key from the fire that glowed in a long pit above which roasted the carcass of a steer. Cut from the drag, the beef was a present from the trail drivers. And now it turned slowly in answer to the attentive hands of a grinning black man. There was music in the night. A gambler's guitar lent weird accompaniment to a woman's voice. Music and laughter in the Cherokee Strip, and an amber glow that flashed from the rounded sides of uptilted bottles.

Mathew and Cherry led the way. They were met at the wagons by the great red giant of the Mississippi, Clark Donegal. He shook Mathew's hand, dropped a heavy arm over Cherry's shoulder and beckoned the others up to the feast. The red beard flamed like the coals in the pit. The black eyes sparkled and snapped.

"Well met, Drivers!" His voice boomed as the rolling of a monstrous drum. "Welcome to the Donegal's house, though a strange house it is, dropped down in the midst of nowhere, no less! But such as it be, make yourselves to home. Eat, drink, dance with the women, and t'hell with the man who's last to laugh!"

"Thank you," said Mathew.

He looked long at the man who offered them hospitality. A pleasant man. A laughing man. But Mathew remembered the Donegal had laughed that night in Memphis when he broke a gambler's back with a twist of those two monstrous arms. A strange man. As strange as the woman who now came to stand at his side. If Tess Millay were beautiful in Memphis, she was twice as beautiful now.

Or was that the word? Were eyes that carried the coldness of ice, no matter the depth of green in their color—were such eyes beautiful? Could beauty live in the amused, yet vastly cynical glance with which she now appraised Mathew? There was no pretense. No effort to hide her thoughts. All that was good and all that was bad in this woman was plainly written for all to read. Take it or leave it.

Did she remember him? There had been no sign of recognition when he rode by that afternoon. There was no sign now. Mathew looked at the glory that was Tess Millay. He'd been long on the trail—too long. And this was a woman. Her shoulders were round and soft and white above the neckline of a gown that had no place on the Cherokee Strip. Wanton shoulders that caught and held a man's thoughts while the green eyes above them widened ever so slightly—then narrowed again as though to warn Mathew against the words that crowded his lips.

A laugh sounded in the night. An impudent laugh that was filled with music. Tess's lips curved in an answering smile as Cherry stepped forward to sweep the wide hat from his shining black curls. Those mad eyes flamed across her shoulders and throat, and the devils danced within them.

"Cherry Valance of Valverde," he said. And his bow was as impudent as his laugh. "And this is Tess of the River— lovely Therissa Millay of whom they tell in New Orleans and Jackson, in Memphis town and Natchez, and beyond, clear up to St. Louis."

"I've seen you before, Cherry—in Memphis, I think," said the woman. "Lieutenant of cavalry under General Forrest when he made his raid on the city, were you not?"

"I was," said Cherry. "Unfortunately I was just passing through and in rather a hurry, or we might have met when you finished your song that night—without the General annoying us both."

"Perhaps," said Tess. She glanced quickly toward the Donegal whose smile had grown thin. Then she turned to look again at Mathew, as though it were first meeting. "And you are . . . ?"

"Mathew Garth of Texas."

"We appreciate your beef, Mathew," she said, and gestured toward the fire where the riders had already found partners. "We hope you'll like Morando's cooking."

"I'm sure we will," said Mathew quietly.

He, too, looked toward the fire. Groot stood close to the pit sniffing the fragrance that steamed upward from a huge boiler of coffee. Beside him was a laughing black-eyed girl with plump cheeks and plump shoulders—round and soft and clothed in the strangest garments ever seen on the Cherokee Strip. Black velvet and spangles, lace at the rim of her low-cut neckline and glittering, jangling dozens of bracelets that rattled from elbow to wrist. Babette LaRoue had put on her finery, and with it she'd put on her smile. But still Groot continued to sniff.

"Looks like coffee," he said. "Sounds like coffee, smells like coffee. Bet it *is* coffee!"

"Listen to thees man!" cried Babette. "I offer him a kiss and he speaks about coffee! Crazy, is he not?"

The drivers laughed. And Buster McGee spread his neck cloth on the ground then looked shyly up at a six-foot blonde with gleaming lips. Andres and Lovelock stood in earnest conversation with two hard-faced girls near the wheel of a wagon. Old Leather Monte watched the cook—watched black Morando as he dripped sizzling grease over the meat on the spit. Laughter was part of the night. It even touched the thin, cold lips of the gamblers who stood a little back from the fire and watched the antics of the drivers.

Clark Donegal gestured toward the rude benches. Tess seated herself between Mathew and Cherry, favoring neither and watching both. A bottle was brought and the Donegal filled the glasses. Then he turned an appraising glance on Cherry Valance.

"So you've heard Tess sing," he said. "Heard her at the *River Palace* when she worked for Frenchy DeLonge, no doubt. Poor Frenchy, whatever made him think a small knife could stop the Donegal?" The red-bearded giant threw back his head and laughed at the stars. "A good man, Frenchy. A brave man. But he should never have lost his head over Tess of the River. Not when the Donegal wanted the girl."

"You talk like a fool," said Tess. Her voice carried an edge.

"Do I, now?" Again the man laughed; a bellowing laugh that bucketed out into the night. He turned to drop a heavy hand on Cherry's knee. "A sad time I've had with this wench. Proud, she is. Cold as the winter. Says she'll marry the first man who can show her six figures strung across the book he holds from the bank."

"Quite an ambition," said Cherry quietly.

"Isn't it, now?" said the Donegal. "Faith, she almost made it before we left the river. Had a planter from New Orleans hooked by the nose—a foreign sort of feller with pockets full of money."

"And lost him?" asked Cherry.

"You might say she did. He disappeared completely."

"With a sack of stones tied to his ankles," said Tess. "And a slight push from the Donegal at the end of the pier."

" 'Tis guessing, you are!" roared the great man. "But wait until the Donegal's pockets are heavy with Nevada gold! I'll take no more of your nonsense that day! Marry you, I will—or wring your neck between me two hands!"

"You're a nuisance, Donegal. You talk too much." Tess turned to Mathew: "This herd is yours?"

"No," said Mathew. "It belongs to Thomas Dunson."

"He's with you?"

And Cherry laughed. "A little behind us, Lady Tess, but hoping to join us any day."

Tess caught the glance that passed between the two men and filed it away for future reference. "There are other herds like this in Texas?" she asked.

"Many of them," said Mathew. "A million, two million, perhaps twice that many cattle on the range. We're the first to drive through to Kansas."

"Why Kansas?"

"We hope to find the railroad at Abilene."

"You *hope* to find it?" cried the Donegal. The red brows lifted in amazement. "You've driven these beasts all the way from Texas and you *hope* to find a railroad? Great God, man—are you mad?"

"Perhaps," said Mathew quietly. "But if we get through others will follow."

"And if you don't?"

"Texas dies."

As simple as that—frightening in its simplicity. Said by a lesser man it might have brought question. At that the Donegal turned quickly to look at the quiet-voiced rider beside him. Mathew's eyes carried a glaze. He stared at the glowing embers as a man in a dream. No smile. No laughter. And at length the Donegal nodded.

"I know what you mean," he said. "Carpetbaggers from the north stealin' your ground; laws that strangle and laws that starve; you're a beaten people, Mathew—and the victors are takin' their spoils."

"We're not beaten," said Mathew. "Not while there's a market for beef. One drive to Kansas—money for wages and flour and beans. One drive and others will follow. There will be cattle strung out from the Pecos to Abilene; thousands of cattle driving north, tens of thousands, hundreds of thousands like a river in flood. Nothing can stop them. *Nothing* can stop them, Donegal, once the trail is broken."

"And you mean to open the way?"

"I do."

"Then my hat's off to you, Mathew Garth!" cried the red giant. He stood erect and waved a clublike arm toward the women and gamblers. "A toast to the men from Texas! Empty your glasses an' bring on the food, faith, it's starved I am at me own table! Meat and drink and a measure of music! Dinky Boy, damn you—get out your fiddle and give us a tune! Play, lad, play! Play for the men from Texas!"

A lean boy with a devilish grin tucked the end of his fiddle under his chin and lifted his bow in the darkness. Music in the night. Weird and soft and terribly sweet—music of the Southland; music of the river. Now a woman's voice picked up the words. Another answered. Then strong and clear and rounded with melody came the voice of Cherry Valance.

"*Chacun vit a sa guise.* . . . Everyone lives as he likes. . . ." A Creole song of the bayous; a song that forgives and laughs away the things men do when a woman's arms are soft and round. A lilting song. A lovely song. And the mad devils danced in Cherry's eyes as they swept slowly over the rounded shoulders of Tess of the River. Daring eyes. Eyes that challenged and called for an answer.

"*Chacun vit a sa guise.* . . ." And Tess was singing—blending her voice with that of the dark smiling man beside her. A golden voice that was rich and round and filled with the scorn of men. A voice that stilled the others as it matched the tones that lifted from the strings. On to the end, then silence in the night. The Donegal drained his glass and filled it again to the brim. The look he gave to Cherry was heavy with meaning—and danger.

" 'Tis a song that never pleased me," he said, and his deep voice echoed like an organ in a cathedral. "A song that might tempt foolish men to do foolish things." He waved to the fiddler. "Dinky Boy, give us 'Killarney.' Or, better still, 'The Low-Backed car'!"

Now the music of Ireland swept over the rolling hills of the Cherokee Strip. The Donegal howled the words and beat out the time with a broad foot while Cherry Valance smiled into the green eyes of the woman beside him. Morando, the black man, sliced steaks from the beef. Sizzling steaks and savory beans, biscuits that crumbled at the touch and coffee that "tasted like coffee." The flames leaped high. And so did the voices of the laughing women. Hard voices, if you will. But it had been a long drive from Texas. A lonesome drive. And tonight there was food and drink and a measure of music. What matter that Kansas was miles away? There was a railroad going to Abilene! Hadn't you heard? Yes, sir! A railroad going to Abilene! And a market for Texas beef!

It was the drivers' night and they made the most of each racing moment. Mathew grinned as he watched. Then he emptied his plate and scrubbed it bright with sand. He thanked the cook and offered his hand to the Donegal.

"I've got two hungry men riding guard on the herd. They'll want their share of all this." He looked past the fire to the clear strip of hard earth where the riders were dancing with the girls. "Your coffee is good. It might be we could trade you beef for a sack or two in the morning."

"That we will," said the Donegal. "And with a few bottles of whiskey thrown into the bargain."

Again Mathew looked toward the dancing men. "You've already given us that part of the bargain. I wouldn't want you to be too generous."

The Donegal's laugh was loud. "I see what you mean!" A huge hand dropped on Mathew's shoulder. "I'll keep an eye on the lads. There's never a fight in the Donegal's place unless 'tis he, himself, who starts it. Rest easy, Mathew. Let the boys have their fun tonight, they'll pay for it with a thick tongue in the mornin'."

Mathew nodded, then turned to Cherry: "Let's go."

"Go . . . ?" Cherry studied the heavy glass he held in his hand, half glanced at the woman beside him. "The night is young, Mathew—young and filled with the promise of better things. I'll stay awhile and take my turn on guard after midnight."

Mathew's gray eyes were cold. They held, just as they used to do with those of Dunson when the herd was south of the Red. Challenge and answer. No words. No movement. Cherry's dark eyes stared back. The mad devils danced and mocked and flamed. They probed at the gray mist.

"Let's go," said Mathew again. The words were blunt.

There was a moment while Cherry continued to look at Mathew. A moment while the lips of Tess Millay curved in a cynical smile. A mad moment, filled with tenseness and a promise of battle. Then tall Tom Jessup walked into the ring of light near the fire. Dust was heavy on his jacket; it clung to the sweat-dampened legs of his pants. He dropped the butt of his rifle to the earth and tilted a bottle to his lips.

"We've missed you," said the Donegal. He spoke to the scout but his eyes held to the two men who faced each other beside the fire. "Where have you been, man?"

"Out for a look-see," said Jessup. "Thought I saw smoke just before sunset. I was right." He nodded his head toward the west. "Chickasaws—a hundred, maybe more. They're wearin' paint an' travelin' without their women. Might be smart to put out that fire, though I don't think we'll have trouble before mornin'."

All this as casually as though Jessup were telling of a herd of buffalo or a run of deer. But the words killed the laughter. Stopped the songs and stopped the dancing. Cherry's arms lost their tenseness. Mathew's eyes lost their glaze and he turned to face the scout. Men crowded close. Women crowded with them. There were questions—a dozen quick questions thrown at the tall scout.

"Quiet, all of you!" The Donegal lifted a hand. He turned again to the man in leather. "What would be your advice?"

"Depends on these drivers," said Jessup. "I don't know cattle—don't know how they act. But if they're like the buffalo you'll have a stampede on your hands at daybreak."

"It might be the Chickasaws would talk," said Mathew. "We could ride out early and try."

Jessup shook his head. "They'll want to see what's in the wagons. When they do, they'll fight to get it."

"If it's whiskey they want," said the Donegal, "I can spare a bottle or two."

"After they've had your whiskey how many women can you spare?" It was a blunt speech. Tom Jessup was a blunt man. He waited while the men looked at the women. Waited while Groot drew a long blade from its leather sheath and tested the edge with his thumb. Then Jessup turned to Mathew. "I don't like to make a stand here in the river bottom. Too much brush—too many trees they can use for cover. There's a bald hill a few miles north and a little west. Would that suit you?"

"It would," said Mathew. "We'll go back to the herd. Cross your wagons tonight and I'll see you on the far side of the stream an hour before daybreak. Might be I can figure something between now and then."

He motioned to the riders and walked into the night. Cherry bowed low to the flaxen-haired woman who still watched him with amused eyes.

"Until the morning," said Cherry. Laughter was in the words. "Good dreams and good night, Tess of the River." And a moment later his voice drifted out of the darkness: *"Chaucun vit a sa guise. . . ."*

The wagons crossed in the dark of the dawn and Jessup rode forward to talk with Mathew. He found him at the rim of the giant herd that was stirring to wakefulness, prodded by the insistent calls of the riders. There was movement along the river bank; a sea of sleek backs swung this way and that as the huge beasts eased into action. Pointers moved the lead steers out, coaxing them westward along the river. The column was formed and swing men funneled additional steers in from the herd.

"You know them Chickasaws are watchin' you," said Jessup. "They've got scouts along the river."

"That's what I figured," said Mathew.

"What else did you figure?"

"That as long as my steers are going to run, they might as well run toward Abilene."

"Abilene ain't west. Neither is that bald hill."

"They won't run west," said Mathew. "Keep your wagons close behind the herd. When they turn, tell the wagons to turn. Or better still, just tell them to follow Groot."

Jessup rode back to the wagons. The herd drove west. Drove into darkness. And close on the heels of the drag rolled a high-wheeled cart. Groot was perched on the seat. A rifle rested across his knees and he snapped the long bull whip happily over the rumps of the lumbering oxen. Behind him rolled another wagon. Then another. Six canvas-topped Conestogas rumbled and bucketed over the brown earth.

There were women on the seats—hard-faced women whose hands held the long leather lines. Men rode beside the wagons. Others walked. All carried rifles. All looked anxiously into the darkness where the Texans rode in a protective half circle. Then there came a long mournful wailing cry that ended in maniacal laughter. The cry of a coyote? Or was it a signal from the throat of a Chickasaw brave? From the west came an answering cry. Then another. Then silence.

Mathew half turned in his saddle to glance back at the scout. Jessup listened attentively. Another series of mournful wails drifted out of the darkness that had now grown a rim of light on the eastern horizon. The scout nodded.

"That's them," he said. "A few minutes and they'll come in with the light."

Mathew motioned to Cherry and Teeler who rode to his left. "Start 'em off. Keep the herd along the river until they're bunched heavy, then fan them out to the north."

"Our own stampede," said Teeler. "Our own *personal* stampede. I hope you're right, Mathew."

"I hope I am," said Mathew.

He spurred his stud forward, followed by Cherry and others of the drive. "Hi-yaaa! Hi-yaaa!" The Texan's cries broke sudden and loud over the rumble of the herd. A gun flared. A second and a third gave answer. "Hi-yaaa! Run, steer, *run*! Hi-yaaa!" Shots bucketed over the Cherokee Strip. A steer lifted its head. A hundred, two hundred pairs of horns tossed high. "Hi-yaaa! Run, steer, *run*!" And they were off! Tails high, heads down, the great beasts exploded into flight.

Away! Thundering north from the river bank; urged on by the screaming riders. Crowding, leaping, plunging—the drag rolled into the swing like a brown wave. Tons of muscle

Tons of beef. The wave grew and lifted, moving north away from the river. A bunch split out from the herd, fanning westward. Still the riders urged them on: "Hi-yaaa! Run, steer, *run* . . . !" Stampede! Four thousand steers in mad flight, and now Mathew lifted a hand and wheeled his stud.

"Back to the wagons!" he called.

The words were lost but daybreak showed him silhouetted against the sky. Showed his lifted hand. One after another the riders broke out of the brown cloud that drifted above the herd. They turned, spurred their horses and raced toward the long line of wagons. Wagons in flight. The horse-drawn Conestogas had passed old Groot in his high-wheeled cart. Cold-eyed women lashed at the heaving flanks. High, hard, brittle voices screamed at the horses; urging them north beside the stampeding cattle.

"Keep those wagons bunched!" called Mathew. "Here they come!"

And come they did—riders of the great plains, crouched low along the backs of their racing mounts. Naked riders, daubed in red green and orange. Riders who carried long feather-tufted lances. Riders who gripped the flanks of their mounts with bronzed legs and loosed a flight of arrows toward the wagons.

Fanning out around the rim of the herd, racing past the stampeding cattle, the screaming Chickasaw braves rode into battle. Mathew lifted his rifle. So did Cherry. Lead answered the arrows—whining lead that hummed across the plains. An Indian fell, screaming a last challenge as he hit the earth. A second—a third—still they poured in a moving stream. Closing in. Riding in.

Guns against bows, lead against lances—the Texans matched the speed of their mustangs against the spotted ponies of the plains. Rode them down. Crowded close and closer to empty their six-guns into the painted faces and chests. *"Hiiii-yiiii...!"* And now it was the Rebel yell that answered the cries of the red men—the Rebel yell that had echoed across the Potomac and through the Wilderness. Challenge of the South—the cry that once rang along the Shenandoah, sounded at Chickamauga, at Winchester and Missionary Ridge. The cry that had sounded for the last time in bitter, anguished defeat at Appomattox was spiritedly used again by the Texans.

"*Hiiii-yiiii* . . . !" Now it lifted again as Mathew and Cherry and Teeler and the riders of Texas loaded and fired and spurred into battle. Rifles answered from the wagons. The women were loading and firing as well as the men. Gamblers, cooks, fiddle players—fighters now; firing and loading, firing and loading. And high on the seat of a swaying wagon a golden-haired woman with green eyes worked at the trade of death. Smiled as she worked, as though she enjoyed the thing she was doing. Smiled with calm dispassion.

How long could it last? A half hour . . . ? An hour . . . ? Who thinks of time when the guns are going?

"They're turnin' away!" cried Tom Jessup. "We'll make the hill—they've had enough for now!"

"Forget the hill!" yelled Mathew. "Follow them, damn you! Ride them down!"

It was grim business. Grim and cold. No quarter to the vanquished. No mercy. Follow them and ride them down. If these escaped, others would know. Others would come and try again. It was a long trail to Abilene.

The wagons were left behind. The gamblers turned back when the Donegal, tired as his horse, lifted a weary arm and gave up the chase. The Texans kept on. Buster McGee had a loop in his rope and he spun it over the neck of a painted rider. Cattlewise, his mount stiffened its short, stocky forelegs. Its rump dropped down and the small hooves cut a screaming eleven on the hard earth.

The rope snapped tight and the Chickasaw brave was jerked from his mount, turning once in the air before he slammed against the earth. Buster rode in, his long knife ready as he broke from the saddle to finish the job. But there was another brave. Another red man who carried a lance. The tip lowered and ripped through flesh and bone and stomach and lungs. And Buster McGee gasped and died.

"Hiiii!" called the red man.

"Damn you!" cried Cherry. The hammer of his gun clicked against a spent cartridge. "Damn you!"

Then a sorrel stud raced past the cursing man. A stud that matched its stride with a pony of the plains and closed the gap between the Chickasaw brave and a silent Texan. Mathew's arm went out. A long blade found flesh. The red man screamed as the knife turned.

"Follow them!" yelled Mathew. "Ride them down . . . !"

And south of the Red River—beyond the Brazos and the Colorado, days and weeks to the south but swinging north over the wide plains—came ten other Texans. Grim men. Fighting men who had agreed to follow behind Thomas Dunson until they met and hung the thieves who had stolen his herd.

They rode the sun out of the east in the morning, mile on mile, across quicksand and marsh and rivers in flood—riding north and always north. Before them rode a bull-chested brute of a man who seldom spoke and never laughed. A man who had said: "I'll find you, Mathew! And when I do I'll hang you and every one of your men to the nearest tree!"

Thomas Dunson was riding north. His right arm was stiff and sore and heavy with pain. But he made it work. For an hour each night and an hour each morning he forced it to work while his riders slept. Methodically, evenly, the big hand dropped down to the butt of his gun and swept it upward while the hammer fell on the empty chambers. Some day a man would stand in front of that gun. A tall man with gray eyes.

It was high noon at the wagons and Morando worked at the fire. Coffee for the sweat-streaked riders who drifted in from the plains on weary mustangs; coffee for the men who groaned in the shade of the wagons while women tried to stop the red flow that bubbled from their wounds. This was the quiet after the battle while guns were cleaned and loaded again. Groot was busy with a shovel, scraping a place in the hard earth for Buster McGee and a red-lipped girl who had called herself Babette LaRoue. He paused when Tess Millay stopped by to look at his work.

"Only one grave?" she asked.

"Yes'm," said Groot. He leaned on his shovel. "I figure they'll be happier that way. Buster was a good boy."

"Babette was a good girl," said Tess. "Inside, where her heart lived, she was very good."

"She had a pretty laugh," said Groot. "If I was young again—if I was a man that wanted a family, I'd want a girl with a pretty laugh."

"Would you?"

Groot nodded. "A pretty laugh helps a lot when a man comes home after a day's work. Makes things go better." He looked at Tess appraisingly. "I'll bet you've got a pretty laugh when you want to let it out."

"What is there to laugh at, Groot?" Tess glanced about at the disordered camp; at the wounded men in the shade of the wagons; at the Donegal and his gamblers who tilted bottles to their lips as they boasted of their deeds done in battle. "It's a rotten world, filled with rotten people."

"I wouldn't say that."

"You would if your name were Tess Millay."

Groot tilted his head and scratched an ear. "Might be you've made it that way. Nobody told you to work in a place where men gamble an' drink. Nobody told you to work where there was fancy women an' fights an' people gettin' killed every night."

"You're right, Groot," said Tess. Her smile was cold. "Nobody told me to. I went there to make money. Money that will buy carriages and clothes and the right to walk through the middle of town with my chin high. I want the things that others have. I'm going to get them, Groot." She paused and smiled again at the thin man who leaned on his shovel. "Why am I telling you these things?"

"I wouldn't know," said Groot. "Unless it's because you're lookin' past me at something else you'd like to have. Something that doesn't mix with carriages and fine clothes."

He turned as he spoke to glance toward a gray-eyed man who was stepping down from a tired stud. Mathew was weary. There was blood on his hands and his shirt was stained from wrist to shoulder. The last into camp, his eyes quickly counted the Texans grouped near the fire. He looked at Tess, looked at Groot who once again turned to his work with the shovel. Then he climbed into the high-wheeled cart and rummaged about in the gear.

A moment later Mathew seated himself on the long wagon tongue and opened a torn Bible across his knees. Cherry left the group at the fire to stand beside him.

"What now?" asked Cherry.

"We'll pick up the herd," said Mathew. "Likely none of them have crossed the river. There's high ground to the west that will drift them north. We'll ride out when the men eat." He looked toward Groot and the golden woman, then down at the tattered book on his knees. "I found the place with the right words. I'll read over Buster tonight."

Cherry looked quickly at the man who sat on the wagon tongue. Bewilderment came into his eyes. He shook his head as though to clear them. Almost it was as though Thomas Dunson had spoken. As though Thomas Dunson were seated on the wagon tongue with one broad hand upon the opened Bible. Cherry walked slowly back to the fire. Once he turned to study for an instant the man on the wagon tongue. Mathew's eyes followd the printed lines. They lifted when Tess came to stand beside him.

"You're hurt?" she asked, and pointed to the damp sleeve of his shirt.

"No," said Mathew. He glanced at the blood. "That's not mine."

"I'm glad."

"Are you?"

Tess nodded. "The Donegal will probably thank you later for saving the wagons." She offered a smooth white hand. "I'd like to thank you now."

Mathew stood to take the offered hand. For a moment he looked down at it, almost lost within his own. "Jessup tells me you're heading west directly," he said.

"Jessup is wrong. I've talked with the Donegal and our men will help you gather your herd."

"No need of that. A day, two days and we'll have them back on the trail. No need for you to wait."

A slow smile touched her lips. An eyebrow lifted. "Are you afraid of me, Mathew?" Again that ghost of a smile. "Is that why you want to hurry us along?"

There was a moment while Mathew considered. "Maybe you're right."

"Then you are afraid of me?"

"Call it that if you want, but I'd like it better if you went."

"Your men might not like it."

"They'll do as I tell them."

"I'm sure they will," said Tess. She seated herself on the wagon tongue and, with a gesture, invited Mathew to join her. "Most men will do as you tell them. But women are different, Mathew."

"I wouldn't know about women."

"Why not?" asked Tess. "Haven't you met any before?"

"Not too many. Almost none until I went to the war."

"And those . . . ?"

"Those don't count," said Mathew slowly. "The nice ones were being nice because I was a soldier. When our troop moved out, another troop moved in. They forgot us."

"Wasn't there even one *you* didn't forget?"

"No."

"What about the others?" asked Tess. "The ones you don't consider—nice?" Again she gestured toward the wagon tongue. "What about them, Mathew?"

He shrugged, ignoring the invitation. "Well, what about them?"

Now it was Tess's turn to lift a shoulder. Amusement tugged at the corners of her mouth. "Surely you must have met a great many."

"Did I?"

"Well—didn't you?"

"I met one," said Mathew quietly. "I met one in Memphis, but she didn't remember me. Or at least she pretended not to remember."

"Perhaps she had a reason."

"Perhaps."

"Would you like to hear it?" asked Tess.

She stood, tilting her head that her eyes might meet with his. Her shoulder brushed against his arm and the light breeze of the Cherokee Strip drifted a tendril of flaxen hair across his cheek. Provocative—deliberately provocative, her lips parted ever so slightly—she waited.

"I'd like it better if you went," said Mathew at length. "I think the Donegal would like it better, too."

"Don't be a fool, Mathew. I can handle the Donegal."

"Can you do the same with Cherry Valance?"

"With ease," said Tess, and she smiled again as Mathew walked to the remuda to cut out a horse.

That day and the next riders swept out over the plains quartering a wide semi-circle as they turned back the grazing cattle. Riders and gamblers and even the Donegal worked under the orders of the gray-eyed man, bunching the small herds, driving them in. Toward evening Mathew and Cherry knotted their ropes and the tally was started. Teeler Yacey and the drivers funneled the cattle between the two men who called the count aloud as the long-horned beasts bunched in a giant herd on the bed grounds. One, two, three and on to a hundred—Mathew slipped the first knot between his fingers and started at one again.

Surprisingly there were few strays. The river had acted as

a barrier to the south and the cattle had followed the easiest course into the lowlands. Tired after their run, they drifted slowly along in answer to the constant urging of the riders. Darkness found the herd complete, almost four thousand steers milling slowly as they prepared to bed down for the night.

Groot was hard at the business of trade—beans for the ox cart; beans and flour and salt and *coffee*! Riches such as the drivers had dreamed about but never hoped to acquire. The wagons needed beef and the Donegal was content to swap; to trade with a generous hand and a loud bellowing laugh. A grinning Morando prepared a farewell feast and the tired men rode in to enjoy it.

"Drinks on the house, and come up to the fire!" called the Donegal. "Sit yourselves down, men, and let the women do the serving. Faith, they owe you the hair that grows on their heads! But for your guns it would be wavin' in the wind outside an Indian's tent!"

Yes, drinks on the house and come up to the fire—the drivers took their long knives from the sheaths and wiped them bright in the sand. What matter if there were red stains on the handles? What matter that yesterday they had been used for grimmer work? The beef was new but Morando was a wizard; the men cut sizzling strips from the roast and washed them down with fiery whiskey.

Drinks on the house and a measure of music! The fiddle shrilled the notes of a dance and worn boots pounded on the hard earth. Laughing women with scarlet lips heaped the plates high and filled the glasses. Heavy beards against white cheeks; heavy hands that gripped soft, round shoulders. Yesterday death rode the plains. But that was yesterday. Tomorrow at dawn the wagons would be off for California while the herd rumbled north to Abilene. But that was tomorrow. Tonight was for dancing, for drinking, for laughing—for all the things a man dreams about during the night watches on the long trail to Kansas.

"A waltz!" called Cherry as he swung a laughing girl into

the arms of Teeler Yacey. "A waltz, fiddler—a waltz that I'll dance with Tess of the River!"

"I'll thank you not to," said the great red giant. He got up from his place by the fire and stood at the edge of the space made for the dancers. "There's women aplenty for dancing, Cherry, and like as not they'll spare you a kiss. But Tess Millay dances with no man unless it be the Donegal."

"Doesn't she?" said Tess. She, too, stepped from the fireside to the dancers' space. For a time she looked at Cherry Valance; studied him with those cold green eyes. Then she turned to glance at the huge man at her side. "I'll do as I please, Donegal, and tonight it pleases me to dance with Cherry Valance."

There was an instant of quiet. An instant while Mathew drew a deep breath into his lungs and got to his feet. The dancers stopped. The fiddle stopped. It was as though a monstrous hand had stilled the movement of every man and woman in the camp. A far-off coyote wailed in the night. A steer bellowed in mournful protest. Then a soft musical laugh lifted through four notes of the octave and Cherry gestured to the fiddle player.

"A waltz," he said softly. Then, spacing each word evenly: "A waltz that I'll dance with Tess Millay."

Rage came into the dark eyes of the Donegal. "You're askin' for it, me lad!" he roared, and the sound was deep as the bellow of a bull. "You're askin' for it—take it!"

It was a fast draw. Almost too fast for the eye to follow. But Cherry's slim hand whipped down with the speed of a serpent's head when it strikes. Down and up—and a single shot stopped the red giant's hand as it lifted into line. Stopped it for a fraction of a second while the Donegal coughed to clear his torn lungs. Then the hand continued to lift. The huge legs braced hard against the earth. The red beard moved as the great chest of the Donegal swayed slowly. An inch, two inches, brute rage and the strength that goes with it brought the gun into line.

Again the laugh sounded, mad and mellow as Cherry fired

a second time. The broad hand fell. The knees sagged. Slowly the flaming beard dropped down toward the hard earth. The Donegal fell. And as he did, Cherry leaped back into the darkness, whirling his gun toward the gamblers. Then the gun lowered and amazement came into Cherry's eyes. Mathew was there, tall in the half light. His gun covered the gamblers who stood with their hands lifted.

"Thanks a lot, Mathew," said Cherry. "I didn't expect any help from you."

"Don't thank me," said Mathew quietly. "I'm sorry the Donegal was slow."

"Then why the help?"

"Your back was turned. I'd have let them kill you if you weren't part of the drive. Now that you're facing them—take care of yourself."

He dropped his gun into the leather, turned abruptly from Cherry and walked to the fire where a woman was waiting. His eyes were cold as he faced Tess of the River. They met with hers, then moved slowly across her face and shoulders, her rounded breasts and the slim curve of her waist, then back again to the eyes that made no effort to hide the laughter behind them.

"*With ease....*" he said quietly, repeating her words of the previous day. "Perhaps you're right. Perhaps that's the way you meant to handle them both."

"Perhaps," said the woman. And her laugh made cold music that danced with the flames.

Mathew's hand lifted. Almost it seemed he would bring the back of it across the thin lips that were still curved in a smile filled with mockery. Mockery of this man. Of all men. She waited, unafraid, daring him, taunting him with her silence.

He lowered his hand, then turned and crossed to the remuda where Lovelock watched the horses.

"Cut out my stud," he said.

A moment to saddle, then Mathew rode out into the darkness. Rode in a great circle about the rim of the herd. Stars blanketed the heavens. The Milky Way reached as a broad path across the skies, streaming north in a wavering path that might well have been that of the trail to Kansas. Behind him were the wagons where the fire burned low and the gamblers were already preparing a place in the earth for the Donegal.

Soon another glow appeared in the darkness. Groot had built his fire at a little distance from the wagons and the silhouettes of the riders showed against the small flames. Soon there were voices in the night—the low, mournful songs of the nighthawks as they rode guard on the cattle: "Sleep, cow, sleep . . . I met a girl in Memphis town, sleep, cow, sleep . . ."

Mathew pulled the lashings of his jacket tighter to keep out the chill of the night. "Met a wonderful girl in Memphis town . . ." He rubbed a broad thumb against the worn pommel of his saddle and sat deep to ease his back. "Now I dream of a girl in Memphis town, sleep, cow, sleep . . ." He turned away from the herd and moved out toward the silence. The stud's ears snapped back and there was the sound of hooves coming out of the darkness.

"Mathew—Mathew Garth!" The voice was low and mellow and husky, and it drifted easily through the night. "Mathew . . ."

There was no answer from the man on the stud. No answer, unless you could read it in the hand that lifted the reins. The fingers tensed, then eased again as a dark form drifted up beside him. There was no need to turn. No need to look. Mathew dropped the reins on the pommel and put both hands into the pockets of his jacket. The horses fell into step. For a time both riders moved in silence.

Then out of the darkness came that husky voice: "Don't hate me, Mathew."

No further words; only the rhythmic beat of the horses' hooves against the hard earth of the Cherokee Strip. A quarter mile. A half mile, moving out and away from the great herd until even the voices of the nighthawks were lost.

"I didn't love the Donegal," said Tess at length. "Never told him I did."

"Why tell me about it?"

"Don't you want me to?"

"No."

"Why not?" asked Tess.

"The man's dead. You helped to kill him. Suppose we let it go at that."

"I'd rather not," said Tess. "I'd rather have you know that the money he gave me I earned with my voice. I sang in the Donegal's place in Memphis—*sang* there, and nothing else!"

"You were riding in his wagons."

"Because he was going to Nevada—because I wanted to go to Nevada."

"Perhaps he wanted to go because you wanted to."

"I won't argue that," said Tess Millay. "But I will say I promised the man nothing. It was he, the Donegal, who said we'd be married in Nevada. It was he who stood between me and every man that wanted me."

"So you had Cherry kill him."

"It may be that I like Cherry Valance."

"Or it may be you wanted to get rid of the Donegal."

"It may be," said Tess quietly. And for a time the beat of the hooves was the only sound that disturbed the night. At length Tess turned in her saddle to face the silent man beside her. "What would you say if I told you I owned the wagons now—that the Donegal and I were partners in this trip?" She paused, watching the play of moonlight across his face. "And what would you say, Mathew, if I told you I've decided against Nevada—that we're heading north for Abilene?"

"Why?"

"Because the railroad's going to Abilene. You say that's true and I believe you. Herds of cattle, up from Texas, thousands and tens of thousands and hundreds of thousands, all going to Abilene. Those are your words, Mathew. And that means money. More gold than they've got in Nevada. I've talked with the men and I've talked with the girls. They like it."

"You'd better keep heading west."

"I'm going north to Abilene."

"Not with me," said Mathew.

"Why not?"

"I don't want you."

Tess laughed—a light silvery laugh that drifted upward to mingle with the stars. "Don't you, Mathew? Don't you want me?"

"No."

She reined her horse close and reached a hand to let it rest on Mathew's arm. It was a soft hand, a woman's hand. Tess Millay was very much a woman. And more than beautiful. Mathew's eyes held to the ears of his stud. His hands were hard clenched in the pockets of his jacket. His teeth were tight and his lips were closed.

"Don't you want me?" she asked again.

And again there was that silvery laugh. . . .

A small fire burned on the north bank of the Red River. Grouped in a circle about the flames were ten men. Some slept; others were almost too tired to sleep. Squatting on his heels a little apart from the riders a heavy-jowled man with gray brows stared at the glowing embers. A blunt finger absently traced a curving print that had been left in the earth by the hoof of a steer. His steer! His herd! Stolen by a waif he'd dragged out of a desert.

Another week, another month, time meant little—there would be a day when Thomas Dunson would again face the man who had stolen his cattle. A day when he would shoot Mathew Garth or hang him to the nearest tree. Until then Dunson would keep riding north and set a backbreaking pace for his gunmen. They'd covered better than sixty miles today. They'd do as well tomorrow if the trace were clear. North through the Nations. North along the Chisholm Trail.

Now Dunson squatted in the darkness waiting for his riders

to sleep. Soon there was a flash of firelight on his gun barrel and Dunson had started the invariable hour of practice. Over and again the huge hand dropped down to the gun butt; it whipped upward, lining the barrel as the hammer fell on an empty chamber. The arm was better now and so was the draw. But not good enough to satisfy Thomas Dunson. He kept at it steadily, methodically, timing each draw with deadly purpose.

A rider stirred, moved his shoulders to ease them in the half-round of an overturned saddle. The snap of the hammer opened his eyes. For a moment he watched the huge gray man at his work. And he wondered what *he* would do if Thomas Dunson were on his trail. Wondered what would happen on the eventual day of reckoning. Like others of the group he'd heard of Mathew Garth—knew his to be one of the fastest guns in Texas. And there was Cherry Valance, Teeler Yacey, Lovelock and Laredo Downs—all good men with a gun.

The rider yawned. Hell would break when the two groups met but there was no use thinking about that now. His eyes closed and sleep walked in to the rhythmic tune of a hammer that lifted and fell like the ratchet in a watch, splitting the seconds infinitely small. . . .

It was daybreak in the Nations and the great herd was stirring to wakefulness. Groot killed the fire and stored his gear in the high-wheeled cart. Tight loops flicked out and down as the drivers cut their mounts from the remuda. At a little distance the men of the wagon train harnessed their horses and made ready to roll. This morning there was no roaring voice of the Donegal to urge them on to greater speed. Instead a golden-haired woman moved about the camp giving quiet orders that were quickly obeyed.

There was a brief conversation between Tess and the scout. Tom Jessup listened. He shook his head and listened again. At length he shrugged and left the wagon ring. He stepped into his saddle and rode to the herd where Mathew and his men were preparing to ease out the lead steers and build the point.

"Can you spare a minute?" he asked.

"About what?"

Jessup nodded his head toward the wagons. "Tess says we're headin' north for Abilene. Says the people of the train like the idea but you ain't partial to us rollin' with the herd."

"She told you the truth," said Mathew.

Jessup lifted a hand to scratch his ear. "Can't say as I blame you, but I wish you'd think on it a bit."

"There's nothing to think about."

"Maybe yes, maybe no," said Jessup. "The Donegal hired me to take the wagons through to Nevada. I figured we'd have trouble here in the Nations but once we got through we'd be in the clear. Now Tess up and changes the deal. Wants to go north and will pay double to get there."

"Why tell me?"

"You saw what happened when we met them Chickasaws," said Jessup. "We'll be movin' through the Wichitas' land soon. They're good Indians but the war scared 'em an' they moved north. I hear tell that Jesse Chisholm figures to move 'em back down to the North Canadian soon, but he ain't done it yet. Now the Kiowas an' Comanches are raidin' through that section, an' they're mean."

"You're afraid of what will happen to the wagons?"

"I am."

"Why don't you refuse to guide them north?"

"I did," said Jessup with a wry grin. "Tess says she'll go without a scout if I turn her down. She's a pernickity sort of woman."

"She's a fool," said Mathew. "Tell her I want to see her."

He turned his stud and went about the work of building the point while Jessup rode back to the wagons. The lead steers moved north and the swing men sifted additional beeves into the long wavering line of cattle. Groot yoked his oxen and the high-wheeled cart went bumping along as a rider brought up the remuda. Trail drive—always the same yet always different. Long, needle-tipped horns that tossed and swayed, jutting from the mean heads at crazy angles. Rumbling thunder of many hooves and dust lifting in a lazy cloud.

The drag was in motion when Tess and Jessup rode up to Mathew who sat his stud at a little distance from the drive. He waited, one elbow resting on the rope burned pommel while Tess moved in to face him.

"You sent for me?" she said.

"I told you last night I don't want your wagons to travel with the herd. I meant what I said."

"I'm sure you did."

"Now Jessup tells me you mean to drive north."

"It's a big country, Mathew." Tess smiled as her gaze drifted slowly across the vast expanse of plain to the distant horizon. "I think there might be room for both of us."

"What happens when the Comanches raid your wagons?"

"We'll fight."

It was Mathew's turn to smile. "With a few tinhorn gamblers, a fiddle player and a cook? You'd last an hour."

"Aren't you forgetting the women?"

"No—and neither are you." Mathew's smile was gone now. His eyes were cold as those that looked back into them. "You're using the women just as you use everyone else to get the things you want. Why don't you try being honest for a change?"

"And why don't you go to hell?" said Tess quietly. She laughed to take the sting out of the words, then loped her horse to where the wagons were forming a line.

"Told you she was pernickity," said Jessup. He rubbed a weathered hand across his mouth, perhaps to cover a smile, and looked at Mathew. "Just where would you want the wagons?"

"Behind the drag," said Mathew. "Tell them to follow Groot."

He turned his stud and rode north. Beside him rolled the great herd moving slowly and steadily toward the Kansas line. And behind, deep in the choking dust of the drag, seven wagons strung out in single file. On the seat of the first, a high-wheeled ox cart, sat Groot the cook. At times he looked back to wave an encouraging hand to those in the rear. At times he grinned and wagged his head so the long black strands of his mustache danced merrily. Coffee and flour and beans and salt—Groot twisted his face into a grin and swung the long bull whip.

Mathew moved forward to join Cherry who was riding point. There had been no words since breakfast. No words since the news was passed that the wagons would roll north with the herd to Abilene. Now Cherry's eyes were bright. They grew deep laugh lines at the corners and his lips curved in the shadow of a grin.

"Funny how things work out," he said. "God must love Texas and the people who live there—even though He forgets them sometimes. Don't you think so, Mathew?"

"I wouldn't know," said Mathew.

"About that business with the Donegal," said Cherry after a moment of silence. "You didn't like that."

"No," said Mathew. "I didn't like it."

"He's killed a few men of his own."

"Maybe. But we had no quarrel with the man. He wanted nothing that was ours."

Cherry's laugh was filled with amusement. "Right to the point—if you mean I wanted something of his. She's a *woman*, Mathew. Too much of a woman for that red-bearded lout. Too much of a woman for any man but Cherry Valance."

There was challenge in the words. Challenge that waited for an answer. Mathew rode in silence. A quarter mile. Twice that distance. It was as though he hadn't heard the words and at length Cherry turned to look at the tall man on the sorrel stud.

"Do you agree, Mathew?'

"That she's a woman—yes."

"And with the rest of it?" Still there was that challenge.

"I'm not interested," said Mathew slowly. He gestured toward the herd that moved beside them. "I've got a job. So have you and the others. Unless he's dead, Dunson is riding our trail. Nothing will stop him, Cherry. He'll come back with as many men as money can buy. He's already named us as outlaws in Texas. He'll spread that name wherever he rides."

Cherry grinned. "All of which sounds as though you're sorry you took the herd."

"I'm not sorry," said Mathew evenly. "What I did then I'd do again. But I don't mean to let one woman or twenty women slow down this drive. I'll bring these steers to market, Cherry. I'll drive to Abilene and . . ."

". . . And all hell won't stop you!" Cherry finished the line with a laugh. "Grow a little gray in your hair and I'd swear Thomas Dunson rode beside me."

"I'll take that for a compliment, Cherry," said Mathew. He sent a spur against the flank of his stud and rode forward.

There was dust and heat and a blazing sun, then night came and two fires sent glowing sparks into the darkness. Two fires, spaced perhaps a mile distant. Beside one a sleeping herd; beside the other a ring of six Conestoga wagons. It was by Mathew's orders camps were made a mile apart. No women or gamblers near the herd. No drivers near the wagons. Four-hour watches for the nighthawks because of the additional danger of stampede brought by the wagons. Four hours in the saddle, circling slowly about the herd in pairs. Four hours in the blankets. It was deadly work. Twice deadly after a day on the drive, riding point, or swing, or swallowing the dust of the drag.

Mathew left no time for laughter. No time for dancing. The weary men dozed as they rode, their mournful tunes fading off into silence. Night followed night and each night grew longer. The hours to midnight reached to eternity as Nambel and Evans, Andres and Lovelock and others of the drive guarded the sleeping herd. *"There was once a noble ranger,"* sang Evans wearily. *"They called him Mustang Grey. . . ."* The words became a mumble as his head drooped forward. Then a rider drifted in out of the darkness—a tall man who sat a sorrel stud.

"Evans! Nambel! Keep your eyes open!"

"Eh . . . ?" said Nambel. "Oh, hello, Mathew. Didn't see you in the dark."

"That's what I thought," said Mathew. "Suppose I'd been Dunson?"

"You still think he's coming back?"

"I know he's coming back. Coming back to hang every one of us if he catches us before we get to Abilene."

The tired men winked the sleep from their eyes. Mathew rode on, circling the cattle in the darkness. Ahead was another pair, swaying in their saddles.

"Laredo! Kinney!" called Mathew. "Swing closer to the herd!"

And again: "Eh . . . ? Oh, sure—sure. Didn't see you, Mathew."

"You won't see Dunson. But he'll see you, Kinney. He'll kill you as you sleep. Keep awake, man!"

"Dunson . . . ?" said Kinney. "You think he'll come back?"

"I know he'll come back."

And the sorrel stud moved on into the night. A half mile beyond were the flickering embers of the fire built within the ring of wagons. Mathew was about to circle the herd and return to camp when the white light of the moon showed two forms moving across the plain. Moving toward the wagons. A touch of the spurs sent the stud forward.

"Andres!" called Mathew. "Lovelock!" He loped alongside the riders and pulled up. "Drifting off from the herd, aren't you?"

"Not—exactly," said Andres. "We sort of figured a cup of coffee might help to keep us awake."

"There's coffee at our wagon."

"Yes, but that's on the other side of the herd."

Mathew gestured toward the Conestogas ahead. "It's late. Aren't you afraid you'd wake the women?"

"Oh, we'd be quiet," said Lovelock. "Very, *very* quiet. We wouldn't wake up a single, solitary woman."

"Not a one!" echoed Andres. "It wouldn't be polite."

"What happens if Dunson and his men jump us while you're busy with your—coffee?"

"You think he'll come back?"

"I know he'll come back," said Mathew. He motioned to the men; pointed back to the herd. "There'll be plenty of time for coffee in Abilene."

"Plenty of time," said Lovelock wearily. "An' plenty of people. Might be that a man from Texas couldn't get even a little drink, let alone enough to satisfy him."

"Might be," said Mathew quietly, "that a man from Texas wouldn't want any coffee if he was swinging from the limb of a tree."

Lovelock looked mournfully at Andres. Both sighed, then turned their mounts away from the wagons and toward the herd. They rode wearily on. Mathew smiled. It wasn't easy. Time and again, riding under Jeb Stuart during the bad days of the war, he'd swung with the troop into town. Pretty faces and pretty smiles. Or perhaps the faces weren't so pretty. Did it matter? They were women's faces. And the cavalrymen had long since learned not to be too particular. A drink and a laugh, a kiss and away—death waited around the corner. But tonight was tonight. And here, driving across the Cherokee Strip toward the border of Kansas death was equally close. Terribly close. And there were women in the wagons. No, it wasn't easy to be a watchdog.

Mathew turned. Then a woman rode out from the camp of the gamblers. Caught in silhouette by the moon, horse and rider moved as a dark shadow across the molten ground. Mathew waited. And even as he waited he knew of the voice that would come out of the darkness—knew it would be rich and husky and filled with melody. Filled with trouble.

"Mathew . . ." called Tess. And again: "Mathew Garth."

She reined her mount to stand beside him in the moonlight. Questioning eyes—green even in the half light. A questioning smile. Then a hand that reached out to rest on Mathew's arm.

"Do you mind if I talk with you?" she asked.

"No."

Mathew felt the muscles draw tight beneath his ribs. Alone—away from this woman it was easy to forget her. Easy to say the things he should. Easy to laugh when Andres and Lovelock made foolish excuses for riding toward the wagons. Let her keep away and Mathew could forget there had ever been a night when she smiled at him across a fire. At least it seemed he could. But let her keep away! Now, seeing her, sensing her nearness, feeling the warmth that flowed from that small hand on his arm, all of his silent promises seemed like so many foolish words.

"Do you still hate me, Mathew?" she asked.

"Have I ever said that I did?"

"Not with words. But your eyes called me an ugly name the night the Donegal was killed."

"Did they?"

Tess nodded, then straightened her back to ease it. "I'm tired, Mathew. I've been in the saddle all day. Can't we step down while we talk?"

Answering her own question she swung to the ground, slipped the reins and let them trail to ground-tie her mount. Mathew stood beside her in the darkness. Again that small hand rested upon his arm. It moved slowly as the fingers curled, asking questions that were clearer than words. A shoulder touched his. A white face moved closer. Eyes that carried the color of ancient jade looked up to his. Her lips were close, offering fulfillment.

"I like you, Mathew."

"Do you?"

"Very much."

"I'm glad."

"I hoped you would be," said Tess. "Hoped you'd try to understand the things I do." Her head moved and the golden hair was soft against his cheek. "It isn't easy for a woman to live in this world you men have made. Not if she's alone. Not unless she's content to live in a hut if through no fault of her own she was born in a hut. Mine were poor folks, Mathew. My mother was old at thirty, ancient at forty, dead before she reached fifty. I don't want to be old at thirty."

"You'll never be old."

"Some day I will. But I'm young now," she whispered. "And I want you." Again her lips offered fulfillment. "Will you kiss me, Mathew?"

There was no answer. The warm lips moved closer. They touched Mathew's cheek and waited. It was all here—his for the taking. This terribly feminine thing. This woman. Soft, vibrant, filled with the thousand lures that all-wise Nature has given to her favored sex. There were long lashes that opened slowly to uncover the promise in her eyes, a subtle vexing perfume that crept from her hair, an equally sweet breath that flared the curve of her nostrils when her breasts lifted and fell.

"Will you kiss me, Mathew . . . ?"

A laugh broke out of the night behind them. A sudden, strange laugh that lifted through four notes of the octave. Mathew thrust Tess aside and wheeled about. His hand dropped to the gun at his hip. Again the laugh sounded.

"You'd have been minutes late," said Cherry. He stepped his horse forward out of the night, both hands held high and empty. "But have you forgotten, Mathew, we've a job to do? Have you forgotten that Dunson is coming to hang us to a tree? That Texas is dying and we are her saviors?" He chuckled—a musical, mirth-filled chuckle. "Ah, me, how the world spins backward when a woman smiles. Am I right, Mathew?"

Mathew lifted his reins and set his foot in a stirrup. Where was an answer? Cheap, small, caught like a thief with his hand filled with stolen silver, Mathew had no words to offer. He watched in silence while Cherry lifted his hat and bowed low to Tess Millay. Watched the smile of amusement that touched the corners of the woman's lips.

Argue? Call up an insult that would make Cherry go for his gun? That would be the easy way. But it wouldn't change things. Wouldn't change the fact that Mathew had broken the laws he'd made for others to keep. His gun might stop the laughter in Cherry's eyes. It couldn't take the truth from his words.

It was a long silence, broken only when Cherry said: "Shall we go back to the herd, Mathew?" And without waiting for an answer turned to the woman: "Good night, Tess Millay, and good dreams."

"Cherry, you're wonderful." Tess's laugh was silvery as the light of the moon. "Some day, my friend, I'll pay you for this."

"I haven't a doubt in the world that you will," said Cherry, "if I'm foolish enough to give you the chance."

Again he bowed. And Tess laughed. Mathew reined his stud and Cherry turned with him. Both men rode toward the quiet herd. Gray eyes that carried a glaze. Dark eyes in which the mad devils danced as Cherry sang: *"Chacun vit a sa guise . . . !"*

Morning, and the herd rolled north toward the Arkansas River beyond the gateway to Kansas. It was hard driving, monotonous and mean. But there were times when the breeze lifted the dust away from the drag and Groot smiled happily from his seat on the high-wheeled cart. There, stretching out before him, as far ahead as eye could reach, wound the moving herd. A thin line of sleek backs and waving horns that caught and reflected the rays of the sun like so many polished mirrors. Silence so still that a man could touch it. A silence that was built, rather than broken, by the solemn lowing of thirsty steers plodding slowly along toward a distant stream.

North with the grass. North with the springtime. Sunsets that flamed in red and orange and blue and turquoise, then a warning rumble of distant thunder and a wind that carried a threat. Mathew gave orders to throw the leaders off the trail. Teeler and Cherry and Andres started to mill them to the right. Laredo and Kinney fed additional steers from the swing into the slow circle.

A dark curtain swept in from the horizon, crowding the yellow light of the sunset. Mathew raced his stud along the line of the drive, urging the men to hurry the tired cattle. Thunder rode with him. The drag stumbled along, weary beasts, some thin, some sick. One after another they were fed into the milling herd on the bed grounds. No sleep this night. Not with lightning forking across the heavens.

Riders circled the rim, holding it in motion, turning it to the right. Groot looked in vain for a protecting ledge of rock or a sharp hill. The ground was level as a table and he shrugged in resignation as he drove his oxen on past the herd—on into the approaching storm. Jessup rode up from the wagons as the racing black clouds snapped across the last sliver of yellow sky and darkness covered the earth.

"Keep going!" called Mathew. "Swing west of the herd and keep those wagons moving!"

As he spoke wind snatched at the words. A solid blanket of rain struck the herd and rushed along toward the wagons. Lightning flared, followed instantly by the racking crash of pistol-sharp thunder. Then a strange, frightening purple light streaked upward from the horns of a near-by steer. It danced and swayed, joined instantly by a myriad answering tendrils that snapped from the horns of each steer in the herd.

"Keep them milling!" cried Mathew. His words were lost but Teeler and the men needed no orders. Mathew turned to the scout, pointed toward the wagons. "Get them away! The herd may break in any direction! We'll hold them if we can but *get those wagons away!*"

Jessup's heels drilled against the flanks of his mount and he raced toward the lead wagon. Mathew joined the riders at the rim of the herd and tried to keep the great beasts milling. Again and again lightning flared in wicked whiplike streaks, followed instantly by thunder that bucketed off in rumbling echoes over the plains.

There was savagery in the scene. Primitive and raw, such as must have lived when this world of ours was being born. Giant forces at work; wind and rain and the terrible power that rides in the lightning stroke. But there was beauty, too. Beauty that caught in the eyes of even the hard-pressed riders of the drive. Strange and unknown, doubly weird because of its mystery, purple tendrils of light streamed upward from the tossing horns. Balls of lavender fire spun and died instantly on the needlelike tips. At times they leaped from one head to another, flaming in a mad game that brought howls of fright from the heavy throats of the steers.

Mathew pushed his sight through the darkness looking for the wagons. A sudden flare showed the swaying canvas tops moving off to the west. A half mile at most—not nearly enough if the herd broke. And now a bolt hit, searing along the rim. Mathew's stud sat back on its haunches. It fought to turn and so did the cattle. A second bolt and all hell couldn't stop them. It came. And the herd broke, crashing across the plains.

It was old to the riders. Old but still frightening. Those in the path of the stampede leaned forward in their saddles and gave the racing mounts their heads. Off and away— quartering across to the rim of the mass. Mathew and Cherry rode to the west, trying to turn the run, firing and shouting and lashing with their ropes at the mad eyes of the steers.

Behind them rode Laredo and Teeler Yacey, crowding their mounts as they rode with fear at their shoulders. Not fear for themselves. Ahead—too close ahead were the wagons. Each blue-white flash of lightning brought them closer to the maddened herd. Gamblers at the reins, women clinging to the lurching seats as they lashed at the racing fear-crazed horses.

Fifty yards, a hundred, the horses were doing their best. They couldn't win. Couldn't hold the pace. Closer, always closer came the herd.

Another flash of lightning and Mathew groaned. A wheel had split and a wagon was down. Slipping, twisting, lurching along as the horses leaped against the traces and the tip of the axle cut a wavering furrow in the rainswept plain. Then the traces broke and the team was free. The long wagon tongue turned at right angle and lifted to point an accusing finger at the oncoming herd.

Mathew swung the barrel of his gun toward the head of the steer that ran at his shoulder. The gun flamed and the steer dropped. Another shot and a second steer fell. Now Cherry's gun was spreading death. So were those of Laredo and Teeler. Steers went down and those that followed charged headlong into the fallen animals. Still the guns killed, building a dam of flesh and bone and curving horns to turn the herd away from the crippled wagon.

The dark wave broke. Rather, a ripple curled along its rim. A ripple that flowed a scant dozen feet from the broken Conestoga. The gambler had been thrown clear of the seat. He was sprawled face down with his head twisted at a crazy angle. Mathew dropped a steer to act as a barrier. No use. A second leaped over the thrashing legs and the tide flowed over the gambler.

Mathew turned his stud and slid the sorrel to a stop behind the wagon. He leaped from the saddle and ran to the tailgate. A moment while his hands tore at the wet folds of the canvas. A moment while a woman's scream answered the crash of the lightning stroke. Then another voice, calm, soothing, promising that all would be well.

"Get out of that!" yelled Mathew. "Tess—all of you—get out of that wagon!"

"We can't," said Tess. "Not now, Mathew. Come in here!"

"Are you mad?"

"*Come in here!*"

No man on earth could have refused the urgency that was in the voice of Tess Millay. Mathew climbed into the darkness of the wagon bed. His hand touched a woman's head. She groaned. He drifted his fingers over her shoulder and his knee touched a woman's arm.

"Move up here to your left," said Tess. "That's Bettymay—she was helping me but her arm broke when the wagon went down." Now Tess's hand was on Mathew's guiding him forward over the tumbled gear in the darkness. "Edna's in trouble. You've got to help me."

"Trouble . . . ?" cried Mathew. "You've got about two minutes to get out of here! They've bent the herd but it may swing back! If it does, it'll roll over this wagon like a river!"

"Edna's in trouble," said Tess again. "We can't move her. She's having a baby."

"*Good God!*"

"I hope He's good," said Tess. "We'll need a lot of help from Him in a minute."

As she spoke another groan came from the wagon bed. Then a sharp, anguished cry of protest that lifted through and above the rumble of the passing herd. Mathew's eyes were turned to the darkness of the wagon. They blinked when a sudden flare of lightning reached in through the parted canvas above the tailgate. Below him, stretched on a sodden mattress of goose feathers lay a girl. Edna—tall, dark-haired Edna who had always kept a little apart from the other girls of the train. One of them? Yes, her eyes and the hard line of her mouth told you that. But the few times he had seen her Mathew noticed she had usually been seated away from the fire—often in the wagon, watching the dancers through the canvas opening.

Her eyes were wide now. They stared up at Mathew in the brief instant of brilliance. Frightened eyes. They glanced toward the second girl who crouched against the low wooden side, cradling a broken forearm on an upturned hand. Then they flicked quickly toward Tess Millay who knelt beside her.

All this in an instant, as though the curtain of Eternity had been drawn aside, and Mathew had been allowed a flash of Inferno. If there is a hell, this was it. Or was it something more? Much more. This was the business of life. Of creation. God's way of peopling His world. A poor, pitiful, wanton creature huddling in a broken wagon while death screamed from the heavens and destruction thundered past on the hooves of four thousand insane beasts. A frightened harlot, if you will. But a mother of men, none the less.

"What do I do?" asked Mathew.

"Nothing for a moment," said Tess.

Again the woman cried aloud. Clumsily, awkwardly, Mathew took the braided leather quirt from his wrist. He reached forward and held the worn handle against the two rows of white teeth that were pressed tightly together.

"Maybe you'd better bite on this," he said. "Sometimes it helps to bite hard when things are hurting you, Edna."

Her mouth opened and the girl's teeth cut creases in the leather. Her hands went up. One fastened tightly in Mathew's hair, tumbling his hat aside. The fingers of the other clenched on the heavy muscle at the back of his neck. Again she groaned and the fingers bit deep.

"Good girl, Edna," said Tess. "Pull hard—hard!"

"What do I do?" said Mathew. Fear was crowding him. Fear of the unknown. "Tess—*what do I do?*"

There was no answer from the woman. She moved slightly in the darkness. Then the wagon lurched as a shot sounded and the body of a steer slid against one of the wheels. There were shouts in the night—the high wild cry of Cherry Valance and the sound of his heavy gun firing and firing again. The deep-throated cry of Teeler Yacey and the cries of Laredo and Andres. Thunder from the heavens and the thunder of the herd.

"*Hiiiii-ya! Get over! Get over* . . . !" Cherry screaming as he fired. *Hiiii . . . ! Drop that one. Teeler!*"

And within the wagon a low pain-filled moan as Edna's fingers bit deeper and deeper into the corded muscle of Mathew's neck. A searing flash of lightning. A gasp from Tess Millay, then: "Damn—oh, damn! Damn you, Mathew—damn all men!"

"What do I do?" asked Mathew.

"It's done," said Tess. "Let go, Edna. Here, Mathew—hold this. Hold it, you fool! It won't hurt you!"

"It's—it's a . . ."

"It's a baby, you idiot! Hold it while I finish."

"Just—hold it?" said Mathew. Something warm and moist and touched by the finger of God was placed in his huge hands. Something that lived and voiced its first gasping cry of protest against an involuntary membership in the human race that had been thrust upon it. Something that frightened Mathew Garth because he was a man. "Won't I break it? Won't its arm—its shoulder—maybe it'll break."

Tess's hands found the answer. They cradled the tiny head against a broad forearm. They rested the smooth rubbery back on Mathew's right hand—a hand that knew and liked the feel of the riata and branding iron. A hand that was old to the sudden kick of a six-gun but trembling and strange to the job of the moment. She turned back to her work and Mathew knelt on the wagon floor, afraid to move, afraid to look at the life he held.

He listened. The crash of the herd was lessening as the last of the steers raced by. The guns were stopped. The cries of the men were stilled by distance. Lightning flared but that, too, was lessening with the thunder. Mathew waited. A little while and Tess was standing at his shoulder. He offered her the child but Tess shook her head.

"Hang onto it," she said and reached forward in the wagon. "I'll get a lantern going and we'll fix Bettymay's arm."

"Better let Groot do that. He's handy at breaks." Mathew waited until the lantern was lit and again offered Tess the child. "I've got to get back with the herd. I'll—I'll send Groot. I'll send him right away."

"Oh, stop stuttering!" said Tess. "It's all over and Edna's

fine." She drew a blanket up to the girl's chin and patted her cheek. "Aren't you, Edna?"

"I'm tired," said the girl. "I'm so very tired . . ."

"Sure you are," said Tess. "Catch up with a little sleep and when you wake I'll have this kid of yours shining like a silver dollar." She turned to Mathew and held out her arms. "Let me have him and get back to your crazy cattle. I've never yet seen anything from Texas that wasn't slightly mad."

"I'll—I'll send Groot right away," said Mathew. He slid the baby into Tess's arms and climbed over the littered floor to the tailgate. "I'll send him right away!"

He stepped out into the night to find that suddenly as it had come, the storm was leaving. Mathew lifted his head. And as he watched, the dark curtain rolled across the sky to reveal a blanket of stars. Stars that were bright and big and wonderfully close. A distant flash showed the dark shadow of the herd against the horizon. Mathew mounted and rode toward it.

Soon he reached the ancient high-wheeled cart. Groot had found a protecting outcrop of rock and driven his oxen into its shelter. Now he was heading toward the herd but stopped the yoke when Mathew hailed him. He listened to the story of the broken wheel and the wagon that had almost gone down under the stampede. He clucked his tongue in sympathy when Mathew told of the girl with the broken arm and agreed that he could set it.

"Anything else happen?" he asked.

"Not—exactly," said Mathew. "You better hurry along."

"What do you mean by not exactly?" Groot leaned forward in the half light to peer at Mathew. "The way you look, must have been something."

"How do I look?"

"Funny, sort of. What happened?"

"That Edna girl had a baby."

"You're drunk."

"I haven't had a drink!" said Mathew. "But I could sure

use one!" He reined his stud and started toward the herd. "Get back there and fix that arm!"

Groot blinked, shook his ancient head and turned his oxen. Mathew loped the stud along until he picked up the stragglers. The steers had slowed and were turning in a wide circle that was constantly narrowed by the crowding riders. Midnight saw the last weary animals safely bedded down. Soon the voices of the nighthawks were blending with the echoes of far-distant thunder.

Daybreak found the trail drivers grouped about a fire near the ox cart. There was coffee in the boiler but there was no breakfast. Neither was there a cook on hand. Groot was busy. The one time he had come to the fire for a bucket of steaming water he had dismissed the drivers' questions with an important sniff but no words.

At a little distance Morando fed the gamblers and girls of the wagon train. Tom Jessup was there, inspecting the wheels, harness and gear. At length he crossed to the drivers' fire and squatted beside Mathew.

"One more run like that an' them gamblers'll have to pull the wagons," he said. "Lost a good mare with a broken leg. Two more ain't worth much. Think you could let us have three in trade?"

"Sorry," said Mathew. "I've given you all we can spare."

"That's what I figured," said the scout. "I just saw Tess—told her we got to hole up for two, maybe three days an' work on the wagons. Got to refit the wheel rims an' put in some new axles." He jerked a thumb toward the broken wagon. "I can salvage gear from that but we can't cross the Arkansas till we make repairs on the others. You'll wait for us?"

"No," said Mathew.

"That's what I told Tess. She said I was wrong."

"You weren't wrong," said Mathew. He turned to Teeler Yacey and Laredo. "Throw them on the trail and let's get started."

Teeler sighed, dragged himself to his feet and limped toward the remuda. Laredo and the others followed, building loops in their riatas to catch the horses they would ride that day. Weary men. Gaunt and haggard, coated with grime of the drive that even the storm had been unable to wash away. Twelve miles a day, fifteen, sometimes under the constant urging of Mathew they had driven the herd a full twenty miles between sunup and evening. And now it was time to move on.

Jessup shrugged and stood erect. Then he paused. The drivers held their loops and looked in surprise toward the broken Conestoga. Groot was standing beside the tailgate and Tess was lowering a bundle into his arms. There was a high-pitched wail of anguish. Then a gasping tear-filled cry. Groot puffed out his lips and stared at the drivers as he swayed the child in his arms.

"Quit lookin' like owls!" he said. "Ain't none of you ever seen a baby before?"

Cherry grinned and crossed to Groot. "Your baby, Groot?"

"Edna's baby. That dark girl—nice lookin' an' quiet." He sniffed at Cherry. "You wouldn' know her. She didn' dance an' show her legs."

Cherry glanced at Tess whose lips were curved in amusement. "Maybe I'm crazy," he said, "but why did you bring along a girl who was—I mean— didn't you know?"

"Of course I knew," said Tess. "Edna used to work for the Donegal in Memphis. She was married to a soldier. He's dead. She wanted to get to Nevada before the kid was born. A new land, a new life—a clean start for them both. She might have made it if it hadn't been for your stampede."

"What's a stampede got to do with it?"

"That would take me too long to explain, Cherry." Tess glanced at the riatas in the drivers' hands. Then she looked at Mathew. "Not even a good-bye before you go?"

"We'll see you in Abilene," said Mathew. "Two, maybe three weeks should do it."

"Then what difference can two or three extra days make?"

Unconsciously Mathew looked toward the distant horizon in the south. Almost it was as though he could look beyond the rim of the earth and see the silent column of riders that moved north—always north. Dunson was there. And Dunson was coming. Perhaps it was this picture, painted for an instant in his mind's eyes that held him to silence. Or perhaps it was a broader, finer canvas. A state in agony—a piece of this fine country of ours that was dying for lack of a market.

His state. Texas. Torn from a wilderness and held together with guns and guts. Built by men who were too proud to beg for crumbs from a savage, triumphant Congress; too brave to run away; too honest to steal. Men who were starving in the midst of a plenty they had created out of nothing. These were his neighbors. These were the men who would drive their cattle north in an endless stream *if only the way were opened.*

Mathew turned again to face Tess. Slowly, he shook his head. "I've told Teeler to cut two steers from the drag," he said. "They'll do you for meat until you get to Abilene."

"Then you won't change your mind?"

"No."

Tess glanced at the other drivers who were grouped about Groot and the baby. Laughing men who stood on tiptoe to look down at the queer bundle of humanity. If they got too close or lifted a finger Groot warned them back. He swayed the youngster gently in his arms. The tears stopped and the protesting cries were brought to a sudden halt. Groot beamed proudly.

"Which did you say it was, Tess?" he asked. "Boy or girl?"

"A boy," said Tess. "Got a good name for him?"

"Might call 'im Stampede," said Groot. "That's the way the Indians do it, so they tell me. Name their kids after what they see first."

"Then we better call him Lightning," laughed Tess. "Or better still—Mathew Garth." She winked at Mathew. "Sure you won't change your mind? You helped to bring him here. It would be a shame to ride away and let the Indians kill him."

Again she smiled. "I didn't think even you could do that, Mathew."

"You won't meet anything but Wichitas this far north," said Mathew. "They're friendly." He motioned to Groot. "Give Lightning back to his mother and get your wagon loaded. The rest of you, saddle up and throw the drive on the trail."

"I'll miss you, Mathew," said Tess.

"Yes," said Cherry quietly. He turned away from the baby and stood beside Tess. "Yes, we'll miss you a lot, Mathew."

"We . . . ?"

"I'm staying," said Cherry.

Just that—and again Tess Millay's lips grew a smile. She watched without troubling to cover her amusement while Mathew looked long at the dark man beside her. Gray eyes that asked questions. No need for words. Cherry's shoulder lifted in the suggestion of a shrug. His lips smiled. But two mad devils danced in the eyes that looked back at Mathew.

"It's your move, Mathew," said Tess.

"It might be better," said Mathew quietly, "if you kept your mouth closed."

"Yes," laughed Cherry. "Let the man think. He's trying to decide whether to go for his gun—or finish the drive to Abilene."

"You're talking small, Cherry."

There was an instant while the smile died on Cherry's lips. Then he nodded. "Maybe you're right, Mathew. But I'm joining the wagons. Do you figure to stop me?"

The words stopped all movement by the drivers. They paused, some with loops half lifted beside the remuda, others in mid-stride. Those in the possible line of fire eased to one side or the other. Silence built upon silence. Still Mathew looked at Cherry Valance.

"Do you figure that you can stop me?" said Cherry again.

"No."

"That's what I thought," said the dark man. His manner

changed abruptly and he offered a hand. "I'll see you in Abilene."

"Yes, Cherry," said Mathew slowly. But he looked past the outstretched hand and into the eyes above it. His voice was low and filled with a promise of death. "Yes—I'll see you in Abilene."

He turned, walked to the remuda and cut out his horse for the day. Other loops were whirling and riders sat deep in their saddles while their mounts bucked the morning out of their skins. Trail drive. Bellows of protest from the cattle as the point was built and the long, wavering line crept north toward the Arkansas.

Cherry watched them go. Watched Teeler cut out two steers and turn them over to Morando. Watched Groot yoke his oxen and drive the high-wheeled cart north into the dust of the drag. At length he shrugged and turned to glance at the woman who stood silently beside him.

"I wonder," he said quietly, "what would have happened if he'd gone for his gun?"

"Perhaps you'll know when you get to Abilene."

There was a quick glance from Cherry. An amused glance. "He's fast, Tess—fast as light. And he's not one damn bit afraid of me."

"I'm sure he isn't."

There was a questioning shake of that dark head as Cherry fingered his chin. "He's a strange man, Tess. He's an honest man. But he stole a herd of cattle."

"Why?"

"To save the State of Texas."

"I don't understand," said Tess.

"You've heard me speak of Dunson?"

"And something about hanging from the limb of a tree?"

"The herd belongs to Dunson," said Cherry. He walked with Tess to the fire and filled two cups with coffee. "Yes, the herd belongs to Dunson, another man who's hard to understand. . . ."

And as he sipped his coffee beside the dying fire, Cherry told of the gray, hard, bull-chested Dunson whose lands reached out along the banks of the Rio Grande. Of an empire that had been built in a score of years by a brute of a man and a freckle-faced boy. He told of the countless thousands of longhorned cattle that roamed unchecked across a range that was equal in size to the average kingdom. Then of the war between the States and the poverty that followed defeat. Men selling their land or trading it foor food. Bewildered but not beaten. He told of the desperate drives to Missouri. And the fate that awaited the drivers.

Tess listened. Listened while Cherry pictured the long trail across Texas to the Red River. The men who turned back and the men who were killed. Dunson's brutal but iron will. He told of the river crossing and the mutiny that followed. . . .

"That was when Mathew took the herd," said Cherry, "and started north to find a market that would save the State of Texas."

"And Dunson . . . ?"

"Went back to Texas to find the men who would help him hang Mathew Garth."

For a time Tess was silent. Then she turned to the dark rider beside her. "What of Cherry Valance?" she said. "Can you tell me about him?"

"Sometimes I wonder about Cherry Valance," he said. "Wonder where he's going and why he's in such a hurry to get there. Sometimes I wonder what it is that he wants."

"Me, at the moment," laughed Tess.

There was an answering laugh, then: "True—very true. And what are his chances of success?"

"Few—very few," said Tess, mimicking the tone of the laughing man. "I know where I'm going, Cherry. I know what I want."

"And that is . . . ?"

"A home and a man and the place in life that is set aside for those with money." The words were as cold as the green lights that lived in her eyes. "Can you offer me that, Cherry?"

"Not at the moment."

"Then you'd better forget me and ride after the herd."

"Suppose my name were Mathew Garth?"

"I'd tell you the same."

"I wonder if you would," laughed Cherry. "I wonder if the woman who stood in the moonlight, not too many weeks ago, and lifted her mouth to be kissed—I wonder if she was using the man. Or if, as she whispered, she wanted the man?"

"Using him," said Tess. "Just as I'd use you or any man on earth to get the things I want! Just as you would use me for the same purpose!"

"It might be that I love you."

"If you do you're a fool."

"It might also be that I want to marry you."

"Then you're a greater fool."

"Would you refuse me if I could offer you the place in life you want—the one set aside for those with money?"

Tess let her glance drift over the man. Slowly she shook her head. "Don't dream about it. You're broke, Cherry. Broke as a beggar."

"Today, yes," said Cherry. "But who knows what tomorrow will bring?" The mad lights danced again in the dark eyes and he dropped a possessive hand on Tess's arm. "Four thousand steers at the northern market—that's a lot of money, Tess Millay. Would it be enough?"

Tess glanced down at the fingers curled about her arm. "Your hand feels like the Donegal's, Cherry. And you're talking as he did just before he died."

"Am I, now?" laughed Cherry. Then his mouth went hard. His fingers closed tighter on Tess's arm. "How many men do you have at the wagons who can *really* handle a gun . . . ?"

For the space of a breath Tess closed her eyes. When she opened them they drifted toward the north where a low brown cloud moved slowly along above the drag.

# 6

TEN riders checked their mounts on a rise of ground that looked out over the broad lands leading to the Arkansas River valley. Tired men who had ridden far and fast. The leader lifted a hand—Thomas Dunson, swaying in his saddle from weariness. Gray eyes, gray-browed, with an iron will that had carried him back over a thousand miles of trail with one purpose in mind. His herd was ahead. Close now, close enough that another day's ride would bring him face to face with Mathew Garth and those who had stolen his beef.

A lean Texan sat his horse beside Dunson—Bradley Rush, up from Houston with a record of six men killed in fair fight. He lifted a long arm and pointed across the valley.

"There's the wagons," he said. "They've been travelin' fast since the storm. Didn't think they'd get this far."

Dunson nodded. Below and a few miles distant five battered Conestoga wagons crept slowly toward a tiny stream. An outrider signaled. The wagons formed their inevitable circle and the horsemen watered their mounts. Dunson ran a dry tongue over dry lips. There was no water on the hilltop. True, he and his men had crossed a dozen streams during the day, each one filled to the banks and flowing over. But the group had been traveling fast. There had been no stops. Neither he nor his men would drink until nightfall. Nor would the horses.

"They're making up early," said Jess Teveler, a rancher from Duval whose lands had been stolen by Northern carpetbaggers. He watched the wagons for a moment then glanced off to the west where a weird yellow sun was again being hurried over the horizon by dark storm clouds. "Guess they're tryin' to beat tonight's rain."

"I'd like to see what's in them wagons," said Rush. "I've

been studyin' sign for weeks, but I can't quite work it out."

"Me, neither," said a third rider—Joe Thompson of Lampasas, a cattleman before the war, a gunman now. "Can't figure why they made camp a mile apart when they were drivin' together. Can't figure why they split. Can you, Dunson?"

"I'm not interested," said Dunson. He pointed to the hoof-marked ground beneath him. "Those are my cattle. The trail's not more than a day old—twenty-odd miles at the pace Mathew's setting. Maybe less. We'll pick them up before noon tomorrow."

"Do you figure they'll fight?" asked Thompson.

"They'll fight," said Dunson. "They'll fight—and they'll hang."

Jess Teveler studied the sky; watched the towering dark clouds moving into formation. "Chances are they haven't reached the Arkansas yet. Even if they have they won't cross with another storm makin' up. She's a big, bad river when she's in flood, an' she's full up now. Best to sit it out and wait. Better than having four thousand head in the river with Kansas lightnin' crackin' around 'em.'

"Do you know the country?" asked Thompson.

"Rode it once," said Teveler. Then he pointed off toward a group near the wagons. "Wonder where they're going, Dunson?"

There was no answer from the gray-browed man. He sat quietly, watching six riders move out from the ring and swing north at a lope. The contour of the ground told him they were following the trace left by the herd. Why? Dunson didn't know. Nor did he care at the moment. Still, there was something familiar about the leader's seat, the lift of his shoulders and the easy way he moved with the horse. Distance and darkness creeping in from the horizon put an end to the question. And soon a thin thread of smoke drifted upward from a cook fire built within the wagon ring.

Dunson turned to his men. "Drop back a half mile and make camp. Get some sleep and we'll make an early start."

Teveler glanced at the approaching storm clouds. "It'd be drier in the wagons."

"You've slept wet before," said Dunson. "One more night won't hurt you."

The riders turned their horses. During the long miles from Texas they had learned obedience was the easy way when you dealt with Thomas Dunson. Soon he was alone, watching the ring of wagons—wondering again about the familiar figure that had swung north along the cattle trail, that jaunty, straight cattleman whom he feared and still admired.

Had he been nearer he might have heard the mellow voice that lifted happily toward the dark sky. A voice that sang: *"Chacun vit à sa guise...."* Yes, everyone lives as he likes—such was the creed of Cherry Valance. A laughing, willful Cherry who rode with his men along the still fresh trail toward the camp of the drivers.

Who knows of the thoughts that danced in his mind? He wasn't a thief. Or rather, let's say Cherry had never found reason to steal. At least he'd never stolen gold or cattle. But a woman . . . ? That was different. And if in order to keep the woman he'd stolen it was now necessary to steal a herd, then so be it. Cherry's conscience was an easy thing and had long since learned to accept the inevitable. He smiled as he rode and lifted his voice in song.

"How many does Garth have left?" asked Seven Phillips, a dark man with soft hands.

"Twelve, counting himself," said Cherry. "And a cook."

"And we're six," said Phillips. "Two to one against us. Those are mean odds."

"Worse than you think," laughed Cherry. "Each one of those twelve can part your hair with a piece of lead at a hundred paces."

"But you've got a plan," said Don Everman, a gambler born and reared in a Cairo saloon on the banks of the Mississippi. "You told us you've got a plan."

"I told you," said Cherry slowly, "there are almost four

thousand steers in that herd. That a steer will bring twenty dollars or more at the railhead. Eighty thousand dollars is a lot of money, Everman. Isn't it worth fighting for?"

"But you told us you had a plan?" the gambler insisted. "I won't back six against twelve unless you've got a plan."

Again Cherry laughed. Then he explained in easy words how simple it would be to take the herd from Mathew Garth and his men. The rule had been made by the gangs on the Missouri border. It had been tested well during the past year—two hundred thousand head of stolen cattle proved its worth. Why change it? Today Mathew and his riders had reached the Arkansas River. Tonight they would try a crossing. When the cattle and riders were shoulder deep in the dark waters a single volley from the north bank would empty a half dozen saddles. A second would finish the job.

Everman liked the plan. So did Seven Phillips. But there was another who disagreed. Tod Ferris had worked cattle. Not for long, but there had been a year when the thin man with the scar on his jaw had worked with a wagon on the southern range. Now he glanced at the overcast sky and shook his head.

"You've guessed wrong, Cherry," he said. "Garth won't cross 'em tonight. No man would. The river's in flood an' boiling over. A night crossing would be tough enough with a clear sky, it can't be done in a storm."

"How long have you known Mathew Garth?"

"I don't know him."

"I'm sure you don't," said Cherry, and he smiled as he spoke. "He'll cross the herd tonight, flood or not. Darkness won't bother him. Neither will storm. He's promised to drive that herd to market and he claims all hell won't stop him. Maybe he's right—but I doubt it."

An hour passed. Then another, and still the rain held off. The tough little range horses covered the ground in tireless strides that put mile after mile behind Cherry and his men. Open country gave way to brush, then to stands of slender black willows that lined the flooded streams leading into the

Arkansas. At times Cherry halted his group and listened. At length he heard the mournful call of a steer. A second answered, musical and mellow in its plaintive note of protest. Soon the voices of the herd lifted in chorus while above and beyond the rumbling, rolling peals of thunder sounded in counterpoint as the strains of a monstrous organ.

Then the moon broke through a cleft in the clouds. Cherry stepped his mount along the bank of a twisting stream that was shadow marked by the budding branches above it. The scent of the herd was strong on the breeze and the horses tensed in their eagerness. Another mile, then the distant outlines of the herd stretched before them in an irregular half circle at the bank of the river.

Cherry heard the voices of Laredo and Andres as they passed in the night, singing wearily and softly to quiet the herd. Beyond at the river bank other voices lifted in the darkness. Voices that urged the reluctant beasts into the stream. There was a splashing and bellowing and the crash of horn against horn.

Night crossing—night and all of its thousand hidden fears working against the riders of Texas. Cold moonlight on dull, cold water. A bronze pathway across a flooded river, then a racing cloud that covered the moon and blackness dropped over the herd. Jargens and Nambel were on the near bank, feeding the great beasts into the water. Old Leather Monte and Kavanaugh on the far side, guiding the oncoming line up the sloping bank to the bed ground beyond. Mathew and Teeler in the stream, swimming their horses at the bend of the U, crowding the steers and guarding the line.

It was man's work. Cherry watched in admiration, held for a time by the courage of the drivers. Once, when a swimming steer broke from the U and started downstream Cherry stepped his horse forward. Instinct, habit, call it what you wish, but almost he sent his mount into the river. Almost he joined with Mathew and Teeler as they fought to rebuild the U.

But there was a woman at the wagons. A glorious woman

with golden hair. Cherry wanted her. Wanted her more than anything in life. And here, spread before him was the herd that would give him this woman. Beside him were men with which he could take it. Cherry glanced at the gamblers and smiled in silent amusement. Five fools—pitiful fools. Each stared at the cattle and saw it as gold. *His* gold. For even now each thief was planning the way he would steal from the thieves with whom he worked.

Cherry lifted a hand and turned his horse. Slowly the group circled the herd and rode downstream. A half mile showed them a crossing. Thunder rolled with them as they swam their mounts to the far bank. Distant lightning sheeted the heavens. A moment to check their guns then Cherry led them slowly back toward the ford.

They found a cove in the river with a protecting bank that would shelter the horses. Leaving them, they started back on foot, pausing to crouch low each time lightning reached out from the storm clouds above. It was closer now. The thunder was sharper and more insistent. Soon Cherry stopped his group. There was a stand of brush near the ford and a lone willow leaned from the bank. This was the place—a good place that commanded a view of the crossing and put Cherry's men a little above the riders in the stream.

They waited. For a time Cherry watched Old Leather and Kavanaugh working a scant twenty yards away as they fed the wet steers onto the bed ground. Keever and Dale held their mounts shoulder deep in the river easing the long-horned beasts out of the U and onto the sloping rise of the ford. Hard work. Dangerous work. The cattle were on the prod, ready to break and run. The drivers crowded close, dangerously close to the tossing horns, moving them along, keeping them in motion.

Cherry turned his eyes from the scene with reluctance. Upstream, perhaps a quarter mile from the herd was a small fire that crackled beside the high-wheeled cart. Groot was here, boiling his coffee into a steaming brew that would be gulped by the wet and weary riders when the crossing was finished. Cherry ran his tongue over his lips, remembering the sharp, acrid taste—enjoying it.

"How soon?" asked a gambler.

"Soon enough," said Cherry quietly. He looked toward the river. Five men were in the water working the reluctant beasts across the stream. "Might as well let them finish the job. Each steer means another twenty dollars."

"Where do we drop them?" asked Phillips.

Cherry pointed. "About ten yards from the bank. They'll come in together behind the last steer. I'll give the word."

Rain dripped from the low clouds. Slowly at first, then faster as though hurried along by the drive of the lightning. The men on the far bank doubled their efforts, funneling more and more steers into the water. Mathew and those in the stream crowded the swimming beasts, holding the dip of the U to an ever lessening bend.

Still Cherry waited. His men crouched in the partial shelter of the brush, shielding their guns from the drive of the rain. There were whispered protests that Cherry ignored. Insistent protests. Only a few left on the far side. Why wait? Why not get it over? Phillips lifted his gun impatiently and lined the barrel on Mathew's shoulders.

"Not yet," said Cherry.

A half hour. Twenty minutes. Then the riders on the far bank sent the last of the bellowing beasts into the stream and followed along behind them. Those who were swimming their mounts at the bend of the U joined with Laredo and Andres. There were the good shouts of men who have worked at a hard task and finished it. A tired laugh. A few words of banter. They'd crossed the Arkansas and were on their way to Abilene, on their way to market! A few more yards. A few more strokes by their tired mounts and they'd climb the bank to find coffee waiting at the fire.

"Now?" said Phillips. "Now . . . ?"

"Not yet," said Cherry. He was watching the last of the

herd grouped on the shallow lip of the river. Watching them closely. Kavanaugh and Monte were neglecting their duties. For a moment they had stopped feeding the stragglers onto the bed ground and had ridden into the stream to greet Mathew and his men. Behind them a score of longhorns had started to mill stupidly in the shallow water. Others joined them, lifting their lean heads toward the flickering lights in the heavens, bawling deep-throated protests. Cattle on the prod. Ready to run.

"Hold it!" said Cherry sharply. He lifted a warning hand to his men. "Don't fire until those cattle are . . ."

The warning came too late. Over-anxious and perhaps a little frightened, Phillips lined his gun and squeezed the trigger. The crash of the shot sounded in sharp, angry counter to the bellows of the steers. Laredo's horse had just reached the shallows. It reared, then thrashed with two flailing forelegs as a bullet ripped away flesh and jawbone.

Laredo was thrown from the saddle. He pitched backward against Old Monte's shoulder, almost unseating the veteran along with him. An instant and Laredo was on his feet in the stream. He lifted a hand. Mathew grabbed it and rode for the bank, half carrying, half dragging the rider as Laredo slipped a free arm over the cantle.

Others were riding with him, Andres and Kavanaugh, Jargens and Nambel. Shots sounded in a ragged, uneven volley from the thicket. Jargens gasped and swayed in his saddle. One foot slipped from the stirrup and he grabbed hard at the horn. Then the fingers loosened and he slid into the water that splashed about his horse's knees. Keever rode in, leaned low from his saddle and grabbed at the fallen man's jacket. He lifted, urging his mount forward.

"Behind the herd!" cried Mathew. "Monte! Andres! Drop down behind the herd!"

As he spoke he freed Laredo's arm. The driver scrambled up the bank and ran toward Jargens' horse. Mathew sent his stud racing at the fifty-odd steers milling on the bank. His gun was out and it flared in the night. Beside him rode Kavanaugh and Andres, Dale and the others, screaming, firing, cursing at the frightened cattle. The huge beasts turned. The river was to the south, the herd blocked the way to the north. They charged headlong at the stand of brush near the bank.

And here, screened by only the slender branches of the thicket, five men looked up to see destruction coming toward them. Five, and only five—Cherry had seen the danger that stood with that last group of steers in the shallows. Mounted, his men could have circled the bunch with ease. On foot there wasn't a chance. No use to wait. No use to fight. When that first gun spoke Cherry knew he'd lost. It was time to go. Cherry ran the few short steps to the bank and leaped headlong into the river.

Now, too late, the others tried to do the same. But the steers were on them. Insane, raging with fear, the long-horned beasts raced through and over the small stand of brush. Urged on by Mathew and his men they dropped their great heads and sent the needle-pointed horns probing into the darkness ahead. A gambler screamed. A second, caught in mid-stride by a half ton of charging beef, spun high into the air. One reached the bank. But Mathew and his men followed close behind the stampeding cattle and now their guns were going. No quarter. No thought of quarter. They finished the job and rode ahead, circling the running cattle to ease them back onto the bed grounds.

Downstream, where six horses stood tethered in the shelter of a cove, Cherry Valance crawled from the river and seated himself on the bank. For a moment he stared at the dark water. Then slowly the mad devils crept back into his eyes and set them laughing. Laughing at himself, if you will. But Cherry was laughing when he turned to strip the saddles from five of the horses. Laughing as he sent each along with a slap on the rump.

Slowly he mounted and stepped his horse into the stream. No need to fight against the drift of the current. No need for hurry now. Horse and rider moved up onto the south bank another half mile below the ford. For a moment he paused to look up at the heavens. The Kansas storm was over. So was a dream that had grown in the mind of Cherry Valance. Almost he was glad. Almost—and as he rode he lifted his eyes to the newborn stars and sang: *"Chacun vit a sa guise. . . ."*

South, a day's drive below the Arkansas, Thomas Dunson had watched from the hilltop while darkness settled over the valley. He'd waited while the storm clouds rolled in from the horizon. Waited while those within the wagon ring had gathered about the fire for their evening meal. Then he'd sent his horse circling slowly down the hill. At a little distance from the wagons he checked his mount. A laugh sounded in the night and Dunson frowned.

There were women at the fire. Dunson moved closer. He listened to their hard, shrill voices. He watched the black man prepare the meal. Saw a tall, golden woman come from one of the wagons. A moment later a scout in leather seated himself beside the woman.

Dunson loosened the gun in his holster. He rode toward the wagons. His horse had almost entered the circle of firelight when the man in leather stood quickly and lifted his long rifle. Dunson kept riding, watching the scout, watching the woman. The hammer of the long rifle clicked as it was drawn into place. Dunson reined his horse. For an instant there was silence. Then Tess Millay looked up from her place near the fire.

"Thomas Dunson?" she said quietly.

"That's my name."

Tom Jessup lowered his gun at a nod from Tess. The women crowded forward, whispering among themselves, to stare at the heavy-jowled man who stepped down from the saddle. A word from Tess stopped their talk. Another sent them off to the wagons. Then she stood and offered a smooth white hand to Thomas Dunson.

"You're riding alone?" she asked.

"Does it make any difference?"

"None, except that your men might like to join us at supper. We've more than enough to spare." She smiled and gestured toward the fire. "Besides, I believe we're eating your beef."

"You seem to know quite a few answers, young lady," said Dunson. "Suppose you tell me who gave you that beef."

"The man you've promised to hang."

"He told you that?"

Tess laughed, seated herself again on the bench near the fire and indicated the place beside her. "You're tired," she said quietly. "Tired and hungry and just a little bit irritable. Sit down and—oh, ask me my name, if you can't think of anything else to say."

There was no answering smile from Dunson. Instead, those hard gray eyes drifted slowly about the ring of wagons. Probing eyes. Questioning eyes. One hand swung inches above his gun. His legs were widespread, his feet braced against the ground like the stone columns of a massive arch. His shoulders moved, swaying slightly as his eyes continued to search.

"He isn't here," said Tess. "If he were, would you expect to find him hiding in a wagon?"

"No," said Dunson at length. "He wouldn't hide."

Tess motioned to Morando and the wide-eyed cook brought a platter of sizzling beef. Fragrant coffee, beans and biscuits—Dunson's teeth gnawed at his dry lips. Again Tess smiled an invitation. Dunson grunted. Then he seated himself reluctantly beside her. He tasted the beef, gulped the coffee. Minutes passed with no word from either.

At length Dunson's platter was clean and the cup was empty. Morando refilled both. Still there was no word from Tess. She knew men. Knew them well. She waited. Dunson finished the second plate and held the coffee beneath his broad nose, sniffing the fragrance, drawing it deep into his lungs.

"Good coffee," said Dunson finally. "What's your name?"

Tess told him. And soon she was telling him other things—

of the Donegal and Memphis and of the tales they'd heard of gold men had found in Nevada. The night was cool and the fire was warm. Dunson let the heat soak into his tired back. He rolled a third cup filled with steaming coffee between his broad hands while Tess told of the journey from the Mississippi and of the meeting with the herd. Of the meeting with Mathew Garth.

Dunson listened without comment.

"He looks like you," said Tess. "Something like you."

"Does he?"

"His eyes are the same—or perhaps it's the way he uses them. He stands as you do, walks as you do." Tess's smile was easy as her manner. "When you talk I can almost hear his voice."

"There were some graves further south," said Dunson gruffly. "How many did you lose to the Indians?"

Tess told of the Donegal's death—told it simply and honestly, sparing neither herself nor Cherry Valance. Dunson listened in silence. Then she told him of her decision to swing north with the herd, of the long drive and of the nights on the trail.

"The camps were kept a mile apart," said Dunson. "Why?"

"Mathew wanted it that way."

"He left you when the wagons broke down?"

"Yes."

Dunson grunted and sipped his coffee. "I hadn't given him credit for that much sense."

"I'm sure you hadn't," said Tess. "And I'm sure when you see him again you'll find he's right about Abilene."

"When I see him again," said Dunson quietly, "I'll hang him." He set down his cup and rubbed a wide hand over his lips. "I'll hang him, and every man that rides with him. Then I'll take back my herd and drive it to Missouri."

"Even if there's a railroad in Abilene?"

"There won't be."

"There may be."

"Then all the more reason the man must hang," said Dunson. "If Texas beef is going north, the trail must be made safe for the men who drive it. We hang thieves in Texas. We'll hang them in the Nations. And in Kansas, too."

Moments ran by while Tess watched the dance of the flames. Then she turned to the huge man beside her. "It's odd to hear you speak of Mathew as a thief," she said softly. "He must have been a strange little boy when you found him."

"He was a good boy," said Dunson. His eyes followed those of Tess back toward the firelight. "He worked hard. He learned the things I set out to teach him; learned to rope and ride and work cattle. I doubt if there is a man alive who can shoot faster and truer. Then he went off to war. Something happened—God knows what. But something."

"Why do you say that?"

Almost it was as though Dunson did not hear the words. He stared at the flames; rested that heavy chin on one square hand. "He knew the things I'd planned. Saw the thing I was building. He knew some day it would be all his—his land—his cattle—his empire. We'd talked of a woman, a strong woman with wide hips, one who could give him sons. . . ."

Now Dunson turned that blunt gaze on Tess. He let the gray eyes run slowly over her shoulders and breasts and hips as though he were appraising a mare or a range cow. "A woman like you, perhaps," he said at length. "You're strong. Built to be a mother.'

"Wouldn't he want her to be—good?"

"Who the devil cares if she's good or bad as long as she can give a man sons?" Dunson shook his head as though to wake himself from yesterday's dream. "What was your name again?"

"Tess Millay."

Again Dunson turned that appraising glance on the woman—cold, impersonal, blunt. "What would you say, Tess Millay, if I offered you half of an empire in exchange for a son?"

There was an instant of pause, then: "Your son?"

"Yes," said Dunson. "You can have a marriage or not. Live

in Texas and play the lady, or go where you please when the job is done."

"You're a blunt man, Thomas Dunson, but an honest man. Would you care to tell me why you want a son?"

"I've already told you, woman," said Dunson. "I've built something—built it with my own two hands. But I can't live forever. Can't live to see it grow. But it must or our country will die! Beef—food for the millions that live in the cities. We can grow it in Texas. Countless millions of tons. More than enough to feed a world, if the fools in the North will leave us alone. . . ."

The words were deep rumbling things that welled upward from the great chest of the man. Strange words. Words of a prophet. And now Dunson turned again to look at Tess with eyes that had caught on fire. "It's all there, woman—the ground, the grass, the water, the cattle. All there, waiting. Waiting for strong hands to pull it together and make it grow!"

There was silence while the flames ebbed and the voices of the women in the wagons were stilled by sleep. Tom Jessup walked to his horse and stepped into the saddle then rode out for a look-see. Black Morando curled in his blanket under a wagon. The camp rested. And still these two sat quietly near the glowing coals. Thunder followed the racing black clouds as they moved in from the west, echoing reluctantly the distant lightning flares. A raindrop fell hissing on an ember. Another splashed across the back of the wide hand that rested on Dunson's knee. He roused himself and reached his arms over his head in a gigantic stretch. He turned to look at Tess Millay.

"You'll consider the offer?'

"I will."

"I'll be busy tomorrow," said Dunson. "You'll reach the Arkansas by the following day. I'll be there."

"Very well."

Still Dunson waited. The rain was heavier now and Tess crossed to the nearest wagon. The tailgate was down and she climbed onto a box that stood beneath the rounded canvas top. Again she invited him with a gesture to sit beside her. Dunson shook his head.

"It won't last," he said. "The wind's changed and we'll only get the rim of the storm."

"Why get wet when you don't have to?" said Tess. "And why lose sleep when you've finished your night's business?"

There was a laugh in the words but it found no answer in Dunson's eyes. They lifted to stare at Tess. Then they turned away and looked toward the north. Unmindful of the rain, the huge man rested an elbow on the tailgate of the wagon.

"You'd like me to go?" he said slowly.

"Yes."

"Why?"

"There's no point to getting drenched."

"Don't lie to me, woman," said Dunson. "Why did your men ride out tonight, and who was the man who led them?"

Tess laughed aloud. "A dangerous man, Thomas Dunson. He's decided to marry Tess Millay and he's gone to steal your cattle."

"Cherry Valance?"

"Yes."

Dunson's hand moved slowly to his gun. He lifted it from the holster and eased it carefully back into place. A moment passed. Then a dozen more. The rain stopped and stars looked down on the plains of Kansas. No word from the woman. No word from Dunson. He waited, letting the minutes build to an hour. At length he cocked his great head to one side like an animal questing for sound. Tess heard the slap of hooves on damp earth. Then clearly, sweetly, came the sound of Cherry's voice as he sang in the night: *"Chacun vit a sa guise...."*

Dunson's shoulders swayed slowly. The huge legs braced hard against the earth. His arms swung loose, like the broken branches of some great tree. Gray eyes bored into the darkness. A heavy chin thrust forward. Then a laugh sounded from the rim of the wagon ring and Cherry Valance stepped out of the night.

"Hello, Dunson," he said lightly. He moved forward to stand beside Tess who had climbed down from the wagon. And as he spoke the mad devils danced in his eyes. "Sorry I wasn't here to welcome you, but I've been out looking over your herd. I imagine Tess has done quite well as a substitute."

"I've come to kill you, Cherry," said Dunson. The words were flat.

"Then you've made a mistake," said Cherry. "In fact, we've all been making mistakes of late—stupid mistakes."

"I've come to kill you," said Dunson again.

"Don't try it. I'm faster than you, Dunson. . . ."

Dunson's hand struck for the gun that hung at his hip. Fast—faster than eye could follow. And as though it were a shadow of Dunson's, Cherry's slim hand whipped down and up. Starlight flashed on the long barrel. Then another hand, equally slim, equally fast, touched the elbow of Cherry Valance. Both guns flared in the night. Two shots and two more. Sound bucketed across the Kansas plains. Dunson's fingers dropped his gun to the ground. He staggered backward as though a giant hand had beaten against his chest. A long breath sobbed in his throat. He touched the red stain that grew beneath his right shoulder. It bubbled over his fingers.

Facing him, turning slowly in a half circle, both hands hanging limp at his sides, was Cherry Valance. A Cherry who fought to hold life in the eyes that looked in bewilderment at the woman beside him. A woman who had touched his elbow just as his gun came into line with Dunson's heart. Questioning eyes. Eyes that continued to question even as Cherry slipped to his knees.

"*Chacun vit a sa guise*," said Tess Millay quietly. "Everyone lives as he likes, Cherry. I've decided to live in Texas."

Then the mad devils flared. Just once. Leaping, dancing high with crazy laughter. And Cherry whispered: "Not even one little tear . . . ?"

Perhaps he saw it. Perhaps—for it came unbidden to the green eyes that looked down at him. Then Tess turned and beckoned to the women huddled beside the wagons: "Help me, you fools!" She stepped to Dunson's side, lifted one of the great arms over her shoulder and took his weight against her side.

"Thank you, woman," said Dunson. "It was well meant, but I wish you hadn't."

"Would you rather have died?" asked Tess quietly. "Or have you forgotten the deal you offered?" She turned again to the women: "Get him into the lead wagon, then get me some boiling water!"

Dunson's head rolled forward and his knees sagged. . . .

Across the Arkansas River the great herd drove north, always north. Eight days. Ten days. Trailweary riders dozed in their saddles as they put another and yet another mile behind them. Twelve riders and a cook, where once there had been thirty. Hard when they started. Harder now. Kavanaugh, Keever and Nambel plodding along in the dust of the drag; Andres, Lovelock and Kemper holding the swing to the west; Dale and Laredo and Old Leather Monte riding the east flank, while the wounded Jargens rode with Groot who swung the bull whip from the seat of the high-wheeled ox cart.

Mathew held the point and with him rode Teeler Yacey—a silent, thoughtful Teeler who turned at length to the gray-eyed man beside him.

"You think there really is such a town as Abilene?" he asked mournfully.

"Yes," said Mathew.

"Couldn't be that we missed it an' kept goin' clear to Canada?"

"No."

Again there was that dubious shake of the head. "It's goin' to be tough if the railroad ain't there."

"It's got to be there, Teeler."

"But if it ain't?"

"We'll drive till we find it."

"Or till Dunson finds *us*," said Teeler quietly. He rode in silence for a time, looking out over the endless plains that reached to the far horizons. "Good beef country. Grass is almost as good as we've got in Texas. Wonder what God had in mind when he made so much emptiness?"

"It won't always be empty," said Mathew. "Some day, Teeler, there'll be cities and roads and farms and ranches. It's all coming. It's got to come. Some day there'll be a railroad that will go clear across to California."

"It can't be," said Teeler flatly. "Ain't enough people in the country. Ain't nearly enough. An' it'd take a million years to breed enough."

"Maybe not."

Teeler sighed. "As for that railroad goin' to California . . ." He lifted a tired, wind-burned face to the heavens: "Please, Mister God, I'll settle for a little bitty railroad that only goes to Abilene, so's I can say good-bye to these here cattle."

Half jest, half prayer—and then as though it were an answering voice from the heavens there sounded a long, high, plaintive wail. Distant—far distant. Moaning down from the north. Again it sounded. Mathew checked his mount. So did Teeler. Both men listened, then Teeler turned in amazement to Mathew.

"What is it?" he asked.

There was no answer from Mathew. He waited. Soon Andres, Kemper and Lovelock rode up to join them. Others of the drive moved in. The riders sat their saddles in silence while the great beasts plodded slowly past along the trail. Again there came that weird, wailing sound from the north. And now Mathew drew a great breath into his lungs.

"An engine!" he cried. "That's the whistle on an engine! A railroad engine!"

He lifted an arm and pointed to a threadlike streamer of cloud that moved across the horizon. Slow, held to a snail's pace by distance, still it was moving. Moving westward across the plains. Smoke from a locomotive! And now the mournful whistle sounded again.

"The railroad!" yelled Teeler. "Mathew—you were right! The railroad's come to Abilene!"

There were no cheers. No cries. Not for a moment. Silence held the group while a slow smile spread across each weathered face. The men looked north, watching the thin tendril of smoke. They waited again for the welcome note of the engine. When it came they looked at Mathew. Then suddenly Keever exploded into action.

"*Hi-yiiii* . . . !" And he raked his spurs along the flanks of his horse. "Dance, bronc, dance! The railroad's come to Abilene!"

And the bronc broke in half, bucking sunfishing, spinning and jolting against the hard earth in stiff-legged jumps. One after another the horses and riders caught the fever. "*Hi-yiiii!* Dance, bronc, dance! The railroad's here an' we're here, too! *Hi-yiii* . . . !" Shouting men, leaping horses, laughter—mad, happy laughter as the riders bucked their mounts.

"Easy, you idiots!" cried Mathew, but he grinned as he spoke. Then he pointed to the nearest steers in the drive—steers that had lifted their heads and set their long horns to waving. "Easy—you'll start 'em off!"

"Let 'em run!" laughed Teeler. "Let 'em run clear to Abilene!"

"Don't you neither!" called Jargens from the wagon seat. "When them steers get to Abilene I want to be with 'em!"

In time the shouting died, or rather, it lessened. The men rode to their places on the line and drifted the steers along. Drove them along. Faster! Much faster! "Hi-yaaa! Go, steer, go! Hi-yaaa . . . git along! Texas beef aheadin' for the market—git along, steer. *Git along!*"

They were short miles now. Wonderful miles. Miles that rolled past to show a dark smudge on the distant skyline. Abilene! Mythical, mystical, wonderful Abilene! Dream city of a hundred long days and equally long nights. Dream city that had been but a name for a thousand and more weary miles. Perhaps the streets were not paved with silver. Perhaps the houses were not made of gold. Did it matter? Did anything matter except that Texas beef was going to market?

Another hour, another mile; the sun rolled up toward the zenith and now the distant city took form. Abilene—a single street set down in space. Wooden shacks that crowded a dirt road. Sod houses and a dozen smoke stains lifting into the sky from their tin chimneys. Abilene the wonderful—but off to the end of town was the railroad. And crowding the tracks was the stockyard. New lumber, curling in the sun. Unpainted and raw, but there it was! The stockyard!

Now there were riders on the plain. Caught by the billowing cloud of dust that moved above the drive a score of the citizens of Abilene raced their horses to welcome the incoming herd. Men of the North who checked their shouts as they stared in amazement at the long-horned cattle of the South. And stared in equal wonder at the men who drove them. Sons of Texas— gaunt, lean, deviled by the sun and rain and wind and dust; tattered men on shaggy horses. Worn saddles and frayed riatas. Wide hats and heavy guns. Silent men whose eyes carried the light of fever. Sons of a lost cause who had risen again to fight for their homeland. Thirteen men where once there had been thirty. But they'd brought their beef to market!

Still the men of the North sat in silence. It couldn't be they knew these bearded grimy riders had saved a state from starvation. Nor could they know that in doing so these Texans had laid the first foundation stone in an everlasting peace. But *something*—some strangely intangible aura of destiny moved with this cavalcade across the plains of Kansas. It squared the shoulders of the drivers, straightened their backs. Almost it was as though they were moving to music, moving in dignity. The men of the North paced their horses to walk beside them.

"Howdy, strangers!" called a black-coated man at length. "Where are you from?"

"Texas," said Mathew. "Bound for Abilene."

"You've made it!" said the man. He rode in close to offer his hand. "Name is Melville, with the J. G. McCoy Company of Illinois. We've got a stockyard ready and waiting. Plenty of feed, water, pens and loading chutes—and a railroad to carry your beef to the East. How many you got in the herd, Mister?"

"About four thousand."

"*Four thousand* . . . ?" Melville's eyes widened as they looked back over the wavering line that reached to the southern horizon. "Guess I spoke too fast when I said we had plenty of pens. Got room for a thousand but the grass is good on the prairie. We'll hold most of them there and feed 'em in as we ship."

"Suits me."

"What's your price?" asked Melville.

"What's your offer?"

"Twenty dollars, and I'll take 'em all."

"I'll think on it," said Mathew, and he looked sharply at Teeler Yacey whose mouth had dropped open. "What's the best way to the stockyards?"

"Right through town, Mister!" laughed Melville. "We've waited a long time for this! Drive them right down the main street and let the folks all have a look!"

Teeler chuckled and rubbed a hard hand over his chin. "They ain't exactly housebroke but if Abilene can stand it, I expect the steers can."

There was laughter then, laughter that eased the strain. Laughter and a thousand questions. The men of Abilene paired off with the riders, asking for information on the drive, answering with news of the North. Texan and Kansan—men who but a short year ago had faced each other in bitter civil war. Enemies then. Friends now. Old wounds forgotten. Old hatreds lost. The Southern drawl and the Yankee twang lifted together in honest laughter.

A million cows in Texas . . . ? Two million . . . ? *Five* million . . . ? You're joshing me, Texan! Pulling my leg!

Twenty dollars . . . ? Twenty-five dollars . . . ? *Thirty* dollars a head at the market . . . ? Get along, Yankee! There ain't that much money in the world! And again they laughed and pounded each other across the back. Visitors who had come a thousand miles and more, and hosts who were eager and anxious to welcome them.

Then Groot drove by in regal majesty, perched high on the seat of the rumbling ox cart. The bull whip crackled and snapped, "Git along, git along, an' take Groot to Abilene!" he howled. "Goin' to sit at a table an' let somebody *bring* me my meals! Meals that somebody *else* stood an' cooked!"

Old Leather Monte chuckled in his beard: "Who wants to eat? I'm goin' to drink an' sleep, then sleep some more. Then maybe I'll drink some more an' sleep some more. When I get finished I'll start all over again at the beginnin'!"

Laughter and talk, promises and plans—the drive moved on into the town of Abilene and long-horned Texas cattle looked stupidly about at the ramshackle collection of houses that lined the single street. Dust and stench and bellows of protest, then the herd moved slowly on to the heavy unpainted pens that stood at the end of track. Stockyard riders came out to cut the herd and drift the bulk of it onto the surrounding grasslands. They grinned to the Texans, and the Texans grinned back. A snorting engine with a potbellied stack sounded a shiny brass whistle that almost stampeded the herd as it screamed a welcome. Abilene! Trail's end for the drive.

And as the lead steers were shunted into the pens Mathew Garth sat his sorrel stud a little apart from his drivers. Once again his eyes swung to the south and held there while he studied the distant horizon. Somewhere beyond that curving rim of the earth was a golden woman with molten eyes. The woman he wanted. The woman he'd left to another man. . . .

# 7

FIVE wagons moved steadily across the Kansas plain in the winding path cut by yesterday's herd. On the seat of the first was Thomas Dunson, born in Birkenhead across the Mersey from Liverpool, come from Texas in search of the herd that was stolen from him on the bank of the Red River. A bull of a man. A brute of a man. Thick-necked, low-jowled, with eyes that looked out at you like the rounded gray ends of bullets in a pistol cylinder. And now he sat all slumped like a bulging bag of grain on the wide seat of the Conestoga wagon.

The hands that held the reins were heavy across the backs. The fingers were blunt; flat across the tips. His head rolled with the motion of the wagon as it lurched along over the Kansas flatlands. There was a hole in his shirt and a hole in his chest that was tightly wrapped with a blood-soaked bandage. At times he groaned.

Beside him sat a woman, Therissa Millay, known as Tess of the River in New Orleans and Jackson, in Memphis town and Natchez, and beyond clear up to St. Louis. A beautiful woman with hair the color of grain that is ripe. With skin that laughed at the work of wind and sun. A tall woman with jade-colored eyes and a laugh that was filled with the scorn of men.

Nine Texans flanked the wagons. Quiet men with a grim purpose. Men who had hired their guns to Dunson for money that would buy them food. Men who had traveled a thousand miles to hang a thief. At times one would ride close to look at the wounded man on the seat. Or to look at the woman who sat beside him. At such times Dunson would nod his great head or lift a hand to send the rider along.

"You've opened the wound again," said Tess.

"It'll close when it bleeds a little."

"Why not stop for an hour and give it a chance?"

"We'll keep going."

"You're a fool, Dunson. You'll kill yourself long before you kill Mathew Garth."

"You're wrong, woman."

The words were flat and cold. The huge man's eyes grew a mist as they stared off across the plains. Again Tess glanced at the creature beside her. Studied the man who held the reins. Was it a man or was it a devil? Cherry's bullet had touched a lung, then drilled clear through to tear flesh from Dunson's back. For a day he'd slept with death at his side, mad, delirious, cursing his tortured dreams. The next day he woke and tried to stand.

It was Tess who had held him down. Tess who had answered his curses. A second day and a second night—Dunson grudged each minute of the hour that took the herd north while he fought for strength to stand. At length he made it and Tess came to the wagon to find the gray giant had strapped a gun belt about his hips.

"Start the wagons," he said. "Tell them to drive—drive fast!"

"You'll be dead in an hour if we do."

"I'll live," said Dunson. "I tell you woman, I'll live!"

He'd kept his word, calling upon some mysterious fountain of life that bubbled within him. For a time he lay stretched at full length on a mattress within the wagon body. Then a morning came when he crawled to the seat and took the reins from Tess. Faster. Always faster. He swung the whip crackling above the flanks of the tired horses. Driving north; driving toward his herd.

Tess changed the dressing each night, raiding the women's trunks for cotton or linen that could be washed and boiled and torn into strips. Each morning she drew it tightly about the monstrous chest. Throughout the day she sat beside him. Always the wagons rolled north. And now from afar off came the same sound that had welcomed the drivers. Dunson lifted his head. He listened. Again there sounded the wailing cry of an engine's whistle. Tess smiled at the man beside her.

"Mathew was right," she said quietly. "He found the railroad in Abilene."

There was no answer from Dunson. The cold gray eyes looked off to the north. The blunt hands held firm on the reins. A lurch of the wagon brought his lips harder against those short, square teeth to stifle the groan that pain called up. Blood oozed from the bandage that circled his chest. It grew a wide stain on the tattered shirt.

"No need to hurry now," said Tess. "You know where the herd is. You know where Mathew is. Why not rest a while?"

"We'll keep going."

No use to try again. Tess sat quietly while Dunson drove. Soon the team slackened its pace. This time there was no answering crack of the long lash. Dunson's eyes looked over and beyond the heads of the horses, reaching out toward the distant city. Dull eyes, glazed with pain. What were the thoughts behind them? The thoughts that troubled Thomas Dunson. Always they had been hidden things. Secrets he shared with no one. But this woman who rode beside him on the ancient wagon was no respecter of secrets. Born with the gift to read men's thoughts she looked deep down into the mind of Thomas Dunson and smiled at the things she found.

"You told me once," she said gently, "it was a wagon like this that brought you to Texas." And then, ever so gently: "Is that when you found Mathew?"

"Yes."

"What was he doing when you found him?"

"He was dragging a cow," said Dunson. The words were almost a whisper and the man was unaware that they had come from his lips. "He was dragging a cow across a continent. God knows where he expected to go. California, I suppose—that's where his people were headed when Indians met the wagons. He was a stubborn boy. I slapped his face to make him talk. He was frightened. Didn't scare worth a damn. He doubled his fists at me. . . ." The ghost of a smile tugged at the heavy lips—the first smile they'd known in too many months. "Within the week he watched me kill a man. Then a dozen men. It had to be done. So I taught him to kill to hold the ground we'd taken. Taught him to ride and made his first saddle. . . ."

Dunson broke off. His eyes went hard and he turned that heavy head toward Tess: "Damn you, woman! What are you doing?"

"Listening," said Tess quietly. "Listening to you tell me about the man you're going to hang."

"He stole my herd."

"Is that all?" said Tess. "Is that all he stole from you?"

"Isn't that enough?"

Tess smiled. "Tell me more about him. Tell me how he looked as a little boy. Did he have freckles across his nose? Was his hair light and burned by the sun? Did he smile then —a happy smile that showed a missing tooth?"

"I told you enough," said Dunson harshly, "when I told you the man was a thief."

"Yes," said Tess softly. "He's quite a thief, this Mathew Garth. And they say he's desperately fast with a gun."

"Not quite so fast as the man who taught him."

Silence then that lasted while the sun dropped down to the western rim of the great plains. Silence while Thomas Dunson swayed on the seat of the Conestoga wagon and grudgingly gave the order to make camp for the night. The circle was made and the fire was built. Soft white hands changed the dressings on Dunson's wound. They bathed his face and smoothed the gray hairs back from his heavy forehead.

"Tomorrow," said Dunson. "Tomorrow morning I'll face the man who stole my herd."

"Tomorrow," said Tess. Her fingers drifted lightly across the fever hot brow. "Sleep tonight and let tomorrow take care of tomorrow's work."

"I'll hang him," said Dunson. "I'll hang him to the nearest tree. . . ." And Dunson slept.

Tess killed the flame in the battered lantern. A moment while she stood silently in the darkness listening to the labored breath of the sleeping man. Then she left the wagon and walked to the remuda.

There was silver on the table of the Abilene saloon—tall, bright, rounded piles of silver dollars. Mathew sat with a stub of a pencil and a square of wrinkled brown paper. Beside him was Teeler Yacey. Others of the drive stood in a half circle. Beyond, ranged along the bar that offered the best in Abilene were men of the town and those that had come in on the railroad. Men of the Eastern cities—business men with money and plans, and faith in the country they'd helped to build.

Call them traders, if you will. Call them gamblers, profiteers, robber barons of another century—call them any name that suits your mind, but without them there could have been no railroad, no Abilene, no stockyards at the end of track. Their morals were few, their conscience was a quiet thing. Rob, plunder and steal—yes, they did all of these things. And more. But they were there on the Kansas plain when the first great herd drifted up from Texas. And they laid their cash on the line.

The talk was of beef and the price of beef. Texas cattle! The first herd was already loading at the stockyard. There'd be others along soon. Real estate! Ground was worth money on Main Street. There was lumber coming in; lumber and nails and hammers and saws. Start building! Build now! Today! We'll need another store—another saloon—another hotel—another bank! Texas beef in Kansas and Northern money to pay for it at the rail head!

And so a town was born. It wasn't planned. No dreamers in Congress sketched its streets. Men built it. Hard men. Americans! Built it with gall and guts and sweat. Built it for profit and built it for fun. It was good to build. Good to spread their country across a continent. They made mistakes. Hundreds of mistakes. Thousands of mistakes. But they'd set out to build a country, and they got the job done.

And there at a table in the raw planked saloon Mathew Garth set aside his pencil and looked down at the square of wrinkled brown paper. "I figure you've got a hundred dollars coming to you, Laredo," he said at length. "Same for all the rest, except Teeler Yacey. He draws extra as my segundo."

"A hundred dollars!" cried Laredo. "Mathew, that's more money than they got in the whole State of Texas!" He looked in bewilderment toward the others, looked at the tall piles of silver. "You hear what the man says . . . ? I got a *hundred dollars!*"

Mathew counted out the heavy silver coins. A hundred to Laredo, a hundred to Nambel, a hundred to Kavanaugh . . .

Laredo turned to yell at the bartender: "Hi, there! Set 'em up, Mister! I'm buyin' drinks for the house!"

"Not tonight, you ain't!" laughed the mustached man behind the bar. "Drinks is free for any man from Texas. So is the food an' anything else you want! We're *glad* to see you, Mister!"

There was a chorus of approval from the town people. Laredo's money was stuffed back into his pockets when he tried again to spend it. Bottles and glasses were pushed toward him, toward Lovelock and Jargens and each man of the drive as he stepped away from the table with silver jangling in his pockets. Soon the table was clear, the last heavy coin was paid out. Teeler brought a bottle and glasses and seated himself facing Mathew. He poured two drinks and the glasses clinked.

"End of the drive," he said quietly. "How much did the herd bring?"

"A little better than eighty thousand," said Mathew. "I left the money on deposit for Dunson at the McCoy Company."

"You still figure he'll come back?"

"He'll come back."

"You'll wait for him?"

"I don't know, Teeler."

The thin man scratched his jaw thoughtfully. "I'd sort of figured you'd make the trail back to Texas with us."

"I'm not going back to Texas.'

"You'll stay in Abilene?"

"I'll wait till the wagons come in," said Mathew. "I told Cherry Valance I'd see him in Abilene."

"I wish you wouldn't but I know you will," said Teeler. Again the weathered hand rubbed over his jaw. "What happens then if things go—if they go the way I hope they'll go?"

"I wouldn't know, Teeler." Mathew gestured toward the riders who were grouped at the bar. "Let them have their fun tonight but get them out of town early tomorrow if you can."

"Yes," nodded Teeler. "I've been figurin' that way, for a lot of reasons. Me, I've got a brother with a ranch on the Brazos. I want him to see these silver dollars—want him to start a herd north, while he's got a herd to drive. I'm in a hurry, Mathew."

"I was hoping you'd see it that way," said Mathew. "You've opened the trail, Teeler—you and Monte, Groot, Laredo and the rest. Tell them about it in Texas. Tell them there's a trail and a railroad at the end. That there's hard silver dollars waiting for their beef. Tell them to start driving north."

"I'll tell them," said Teeler quietly. "An' maybe I'll tell them about Mathew Garth who opened the trail to Kansas."

He finished his drink and stood, then he rested his hands on the pockets of his jacket that were bulging with silver. For a moment he looked down at the gray-eyed man at the table. Twice he opened his mouth to speak. Each time he changed his mind. At length he turned and walked to the bar.

And, almost as though she had been waiting for the chair to empty, Tess Millay entered the room and seated herself opposite Mathew. A red-faced man at the bar turned with a drink in his hand. He smiled at Tess and started toward her. Teeler Yacey stepped in his way.

"I wouldn't," said Teeler. His smile was friendly but filled with meaning. "I wouldn't, Mister."

The red-faced man looked again at Tess. Looked at the man who faced her across the table. He grinned and hooked an arm under Teeler's elbow: "Let's you an' me have a drink, Texan." And both men turned to face the bartender.

"So you found the railroad," said Tess. "Found a market for Texas beef."

"Is Cherry with you?" asked Mathew.

"Cherry is dead," said Tess. "Dunson killed him before we crossed the Arkansas."

"I'm sorry," said Mathew quietly. "I liked Cherry Valance."

"He tried to steal your herd."

"I figured he'd try and I wasn't surprised when he did. But that's your fault, not his."

"You'd have tried to kill him if he came to Abilene."

"That still doesn't mean I don't like him."

Tess smiled. It was a thin smile that told of her amazement. "You're a strange man, Mathew Garth. I wonder why I want to keep you alive?"

"Do you?"

"Very much," said Tess. "So much that I've come tonight to tell you Dunson and his men will be here tomorrow. If they start at sunup the wagons should reach here before noon."

"He's riding with you?"

"He's asked me to marry him," said Tess. "I've said that I will."

"That was smart," said Mathew. The words were flat as the table top. "There's better than eighty thousand dollars waiting for him at the stockyard. If he markets the rest of the cattle on his range he'll get ten times that, maybe more. You've made a good gamble, Tess."

"I'll throw it away if you'll leave Abilene."

There was an instant while the gray eyes reached far into the jade depths. An instant while Tess of the River called up every womanly charm that had sent men mad from New Orleans to St. Louis. A half smile, lips that rounded in promise, eyes that told of the many things that were Mathew Garth's for the taking. She leaned closer, reached her hand across the table top to let it rest upon his. And as she saw a dull mist grow over the eyes that looked back into hers, a single tear came unbidden to wait upon her cheek.

"I love you," she said. As simple as that. "I love you, Mathew Garth. I've never loved another man. I never will. Let's go away—somewhere—anywhere! Ride west and I'll follow you. There's gold in Nevada—gold and happiness and a warm sun that shines all the year. Don't wait for Dunson. *Don't wait to be killed!*"

"When you see him tonight," said Mathew, "tell him I'll be here. Tell him the man who stole his herd is waiting in Abilene."

"Don't you want me, Mathew?"

"Not if you belong to Dunson."

Green flames swirled in her eyes as Tess pushed back her chair. Words were on her lips, a dozen angry words. But why argue? Why fight against the inevitable? Why play with biting phrases when everything within you is screaming in protest? Sometimes truth helps. Tess tried it now.

"I want you, Mathew," she said softly. "Perhaps that's not important. Perhaps it doesn't mean anything. But whatever is good in Tess Millay is yours if you'll have it. There's little I want in return—almost nothing. A smile. An occasional touch of your hand. Because I've found that loving is giving, Mathew—not taking." She paused and her lips fought for a smile. "Maybe that's why I'm making such a bad job of the telling. Giving is something I've never done before. Won't you take what I offer? Won't you take my life, and your life along with it?"

There was no answer from the man at the table. Tess turned, walked to the door and stepped into the night. Alone, Mathew reached for the bottle Teeler Yacey had left on the table. He tilted it, spilling the brown liquid into a tall glass. He lifted the brimming rim to his lips and drank.

And when it was high noon in Abilene Mathew Garth still sat at the table. The bottle was empty, so was the glass. The hands had walked slowly around the ancient clock behind the bar. A swamper drifted the stump of a broom across the littered floor. All night at the table alone. All night, and not a word from the gray-eyed man. He had been silent while laughter swirled about him. Silent when sometimes the laughter changed to angry words that lead to flailing fists. A quiet man alone at a table.

One after another his riders had come to shake his hand and wish him well. He'd listened to their plans—how Laredo was heading south to gather a herd and try the trail again, how Andres and Lovelock were pooling their dollars to buy some cows while the market was down. He listened while Groot told of the Easterner who was building a restaurant here on the main street, and with Groot as his partner planned to make a quick fortune. Dreams and plans, then they shook his hand and said good-bye.

And now they were all gone and it was high noon in Abilene. Melville, the broker, came in from the single narrow street. For a moment he paused while his eyes probed through the half light of the deserted bar. When he saw Mathew he crossed to stand at the table beside him. He dropped a hand on the seated man's shoulder.

"There are some men outside," he said, and the words were troubled. "Mounted men from Texas and five wagons. There's a Thomas Dunson who says he wants to see you."

"I'll be right there," said Mathew slowly.

"Are you sure you're all right?"

"Yes."

"Is there anything I can do?"

"Yes," said Mathew again. He looked up at Melville and smiled. "Tell him I'll be right there."

Melville left. Mathew pushed the empty bottle aside. He stood, rubbed the haze from his eyes and drew a deep breath into his lungs. A hand dropped down to the heavy belt that hung at his waist. Almost without direction the fingers loosened the gun in its holster. He ran a dry tongue over equally dry lips. He looked at the clock, then turned and walked slowly toward the door.

The wagons were there, drawn in a long line behind the mounted men. Hard men who watched Mathew come onto the low verandah that was only a single step above the wooden sidewalk. He closed his eyes, then let them open slowly as they adjusted themselves to the mad glare of the sun. Yes, there were the wagons. And on the wide seat of the first sat a monstrous man. Beside him was a woman who had twice, within twenty-four hours, gone down to defeat beneath the will of two men.

Tess had tried. Throughout the night and all through the morning she had tried to change the will of Thomas Dunson. She'd talked, she'd coaxed, she'd threatened and promised. All to no avail. With the first light of morning Dunson had reached for his gun. Even as Tess had changed the sodden bandage above the wound, he'd strapped the wide belt about his waist and given the order that sent the wagons rolling into Abilene.

Now they were here. And facing them, Mathew Garth stood alone. He stared at Dunson, then let his eyes run over the faces of the mounted men who had traveled a thousand miles on an errand of death. There was a moment of silence. Then the slow, rhythmic tread of horses' hooves sounded from the far end of the street.

Mathew turned. There, sitting their mounts with deceptive ease, were Teeler Yacey and the riders of the drive. One step after another they walked their mustangs on toward the group near the wagons. Teeler Yacey lifted a hand. The horses stopped. There were no words. But each man's hand hung inches above a loosened gun. They waited.

"I thought you'd started for Texas," said Mathew quietly. "I *asked* you to start for Texas."

"We figured we'd wait a while," said Teeler. He looked toward the mounted men near the wagons. "After these fellers had ridden a thousand miles we didn't want to disappoint them."

Tension crackled in the warm breeze that flowed through the street in Abilene. There were eyes that were bright with challenge. Hands that were rigid, with fingers crooked and ready. A falling leaf would have started the guns roaring. Anything, or nothing, if it lasted another dozen seconds. But slowly, wearily, Mathew shook his head. His hands well above his guns he stepped forward to the rim of the verandah.

"No, Teeler—no!" And he turned to face the men near the wagons. "You men have no quarrel with these riders of mine. You're Texans. So are they—honest men who worked for wages. They meant no wrong. They've *done* no wrong. The herd is at the stockyard and eighty thousand dollars is waiting for its owner. I tell you again, you have no quarrel."

"I have," said a deep voice from the lead wagon. Thomas Dunson handed the reins to the woman who sat beside him. "I have a quarrel with any man who would steal a herd."

"You've found that man," said Mathew. "Do you need ten men at your back to face me?"

"Ten men at my back . . . ?" Dunson stood, thrusting his heavy legs hard against the wagon floor. "I'll face you alone, and well you know it, Mathew Garth!"

Dunson crossed to the wagon edge. He grasped the side with one hand and turned to step over the wheel. His foot reached for the iron hub. He paused. Those heavy lips pressed hard to hold back a groan. There was fresh blood on the bandage. Blood that oozed along the cloth as he put his weight on the wheel hub. Another long reach toward the ground and a film of whiteness spread under the leather of his face. Dunson swayed as he stood—strength and life itself were bubbling out of his wound.

"Let me help you!" said Tess. She moved to step over the wheel. "Let me stand by your side!"

"Stay where you are, woman," said Dunson. "I saw you stand at another man's side."

He turned to look across toward the verandah. There were no words from the men. No sound. No movement by the riders or the horses they sat. The citizens of Abilene, sensing death in the air, had withdrawn to the street ends. Now the gray man released his hold on the wagon. He steadied himself. With an effort he stood erect. Both hands swung like those of some giant ape. One step. Then another. A rasping breath was drawn deep into the great lungs through flaring nostrils. Another step. One more . . .

And on the verandah that was just above the wooden sidewalk stood Mathew Garth. Both arms hung loose. His feet were thrust hard against the boards in the stance he had learned from Thomas Dunson. His head was up. Those cold gray eyes held steadily on the figure that came slowly toward him. Gray on gray. Challenge and answer.

"I'm going to kill you, Mathew."

It was simply said, but each word carried the certain promise of death. Another step. Another rasping breath. Dunson's head lowered like that of a bull in rage. Cold rage. It lived in the glazed, leaden eyes. And still another step. The huge body swayed. Ponderous, monstrous, a brute of a man carried forward by an iron will. There was blood on the shirt front, now. A stain that spread wetly down toward the heavy belt that sagged at his waist. There was blood on the dust of the road. Another breath—one that throbbed as it distended the tortured chest.

"I'm going to kill you, Mathew," he said again.

Each finger of Mathew's hand opened wide, thrusting outward like the spokes of a wagon wheel. This, too, he had learned from Dunson. The hand was held inches above his gun. His eyes locked with those of the man who had taught him to draw. Taught him to kill. Waiting, watching, probing for the sign that tells that death is on the way. Still there was no movement. Silence crowded down upon the street in Abilene.

"Draw!" cried Dunson. "Draw, damn you!"

And with the words the great hand swept toward the gun. Fast—yet not so fast as in other days. Fever and pain and age—weakness that grows when a man's blood slips away through a gaping wound—all these had stolen the speed from a hand that was once the fastest in Texas. Slowed a draw that could no longer match that of the younger man who faced him.

Down and up, Mathew lifted the long barrel in a sweeping draw that tilted the gun muzzle inches above the line of fire. A single swift snap of the wrist and the sights would come to bear. But the gun hung—hung at an angle as though some unseen hand had fastened its grip on Mathew's wrist. Veins throbbed in the man's neck, straining, twisting, scarlet veins that leaped and pulsed. His lips flattened and pulled away from the white teeth beneath them. Still the gun hung.

Not Dunson's. The barrel went up in an identical draw and the heavy wrist snapped it into line. The huge man pushed his sight through the curtain of weakness that clouded the gray eyes. Pressure on the trigger. Sound hammered against the silence. It bucketed along the street waking the echoes of a woman's scream. Mathew's shoulders rocked as the lead found its mark. Stunned for an instant, his head wavered. Still the gun hung. Still the barrel was lifted above the line of fire.

Dunson fired again. A clear miss that tore splinters from a verandah post. A third shot—wider now, shattering a window glass in the saloon. Mathew stood, swaying like a tall tree that is touched by the wind. His eyes were wide. Cold. Staring things. Sweat beaded his forehead and twisted in tiny streams along his lean jaws. Still the gun hung.

Dunson drew a sobbing breath. His gun hand wavered as he tried to bring it into line. The great knees bent. Lunging forward, calling on his last spasm of strength, he hurled the gun at Mathew Garth and crashed forward onto the dust of the road.

Mathew's arm lowered. Slowly, as though the muscles were reluctant to fight against the power that had cramped them—slowly the hand dropped down to slip the gun into its holster. He touched his lips with a dry tongue and stepped forward, placing each foot carefully. His eyes held in bewilderment on the massive figure that was sprawled on the ground. They looked at the blood-soaked shirt and the red stain that was clotting the dust. As a man in a dream he watched a golden-haired woman run from the wagon. He stood stupidly, dazed and silent as Tess knelt beside the fallen giant.

"Fools! Fools!" she cried. "Madmen—both of you! Mathew! Stop staring and get a doctor!"

Mathew nodded, then turned and stumbled into the arms of Teeler Yacey.

An early moon saw a single wagon rolling south—south across the Nations, bound for Texas and the banks of the Rio Grande. A single wagon driven by a silent, gray-eyed man who moved at times to ease a bandaged shoulder. There were voices within the wagon. Or rather, a single deep voice that refused to be stilled. Thomas Dunson was stretched on a bed that was lashed to the wagon floor. A shell of a man who had wrestled with death and refused to concede a victory. A willful man who had roared down the warnings of a doctor brought in on the railroad.

He couldn't live, the doctor said. Couldn't possibly last a week if he held to this mad scheme. A thousand miles and more in a wagon . . . ? No man born of woman could make that trip with a torn lung and a bleeding chest. Here in Abilene there was a chance. If he lasted a week they'd move him by train to a hospital in a larger city. But a wagon trip to Texas—it couldn't be done.

"I'll live," said Dunson. "I'll keep alive to see Texas again and all hell won't stop me!"

"You're a fool, Dunson," said Tess.

"Stop talking, woman!"

And Tess had stopped. Now she sat in the wagon beside the willful man who lifted a weak hand to brush away the white fingers that had been laid across his lips. A blunt thumb pointed forward toward the opening of the canvas above the driver's seat.

"Where are we now?" asked Dunson.

"Close," said Tess. "The Red River is just ahead. Beyond that is Texas."

"Tell him to hurry."

"You'll open your wound."

"Damn the wound, woman!" said Dunson. "It hasn't been closed since the day I got it. Tell Mathew to hurry."

"He won't drive faster," said Tess. "He wants you to live."

"That's because he's soft," said Dunson. "He's soft, Tess. I've always worried about that."

"Have you?"

"You'll have to breed the hardness into that son of yours." Dull gray eyes looked up into the green ones above them. "I won't have a lot of soft brats running around the place when I'm gone. Won't have 'em!"

"You're not going anywhere, and you talk too much," smiled Tess. Again the white fingers rested across the heavy lips. "And you forget that Mathew hasn't said anything about breeding any brats."

"*He'll do as I say!*" The words were an echo of the voice that once roared like a bull. "*He'll do as I say or . . .*"

"Or you'll hang him," said Tess. Her smile was soft as her voice. "You're a hard man, Thomas Dunson."

Mathew checked the team and looked back from the driver's seat. "We've reached the Red River. We'll camp here tonight and cross in the morning."

"Cross tonight," said Dunson. "Cross now!"

Something in his voice took the smile from Tess's lips. Something different. Something that had grown with the miles nd had now reached a zenith. She looked forward. Mathew ad heard it, too. He nodded once, then turned and lifted the eins. The long lash cracked over the rumps of the tired horses nd they moved forward into the stream.

It was down now. But even at the ford the water crept bove the wheel hubs and flowed into the bed of the wagon. Dunson turned his head. He dropped a hand to let the blunt ngers trail in the muddy water. He touched his lips and isted the earth that was carried by the stream. When the agon stopped on the far bank and Mathew came to the tail- ate, Dunson braced himself on the bed.

"Lift me out, Mathew," he said.

There was no word of argument. Mathew crouched above he bed and cradled the huge man in his arms. Bending, easing ne foot after another he walked to the back of the wagon. Dunson's teeth snapped shut above a groan as Mathew climbed o the ground.

"I'll stand," he said. "Set me down."

Mathew lowered his feet to the earth. Dunson reached gain deep down into that iron will and found the strength o stand erect. He looked south over the moonswept plain. He lifted an arm.

"That's Texas, Mathew," he said slowly. "I've come home."

"You've come home," said Mathew.

Quietly, like a man who lies down to pleasant dreams, Thomas Dunson slipped to the ground. His great arms stretched ut and he pillowed his face on the earth he loved so well. And as he died, he smiled.

That night Mathew and Tess made camp beside the rough ile of stones that marked Dunson's place beside the Red River. Bright with the sunrise the Conestoga wagon rumbled slowly long over the trail that in a few short years brought four million head of Texas cattle to the Northern markets. South in he promise of a new day. South, into the break of the dawn.

This Bantam book contains the complete text of the original edition. Not one word has been changed or omitted. The low-priced Bantam edition is made possible by the large sale and effective promotion of the original edition, published by Random House, Inc., under the title *Blazing Guns on the Chisholm Trail*.

# THEY BRANDED HIM— OUTLAW!

**"IT'S NEVER RIGHT TO RIDE THE BADLANDS, KID..."**

But Chance Pagan had no other choice. He was an outlaw now, a cattle thief, accused of dry-gulching the man who had raised him.

**"THEY'LL CLASS YOU WITH THE WILD BUNCH..."**

But Chance Pagan wouldn't walk into a jail that promised him only a hanging. No, it had to be the Badlands, the outlaw-infested Badlands where a man might clear his name—if he lived long enough.

Bennett Foster, snap-shooting author of Bantam's *Trigger Kid* and *Barbed Wire* is back again, with a smashing ride into the land of lawless men, into the Badlands.

### WATCH FOR **BADLANDS** BY **BENNETT FOSTER**
*wherever Bantam Books are sold.*

## Have You Read These
# Bantam Best-Sellers

You can get the popular mysteries, novels, books of humor and non-fiction listed just below through the dealer from whom you bought this Bantam Book. And, in another list, further on, you'll find famous books no longer at dealers but available to you for a limited time directly from the publisher.

- 3. "NEVADA," Zane Grey, *Western*
- 5. SCARAMOUCHE, Rafael Sabatini, *novel*
- 8. THE GREAT GATSBY, F. Scott Fitzgerald, *novel*
- 22. BABBITT, Sinclair Lewis, *novel*
- 26. NET OF COBWEBS, Elisabeth Sanxay Holding, *mystery*
- 48. THE LAUGHTER OF MY FATHER, Carlos Bulosan, *humor*
- 75. CANNERY ROW, John Steinbeck, *novel*
- 100. THE CAUTIOUS AMORIST, Norman Lindsay, *novel*
- 112. HARDCASE, Luke Short, *Western*
- 116. GREAT STORIES FROM THE SATURDAY EVENING POST, Ben Hibbs, editor
- 121. MY MAN GODFREY, Eric Hatch, *humorous novel*
- 122. A CERTAIN DOCTOR FRENCH, Elizabeth Seifert, *romance*
- 124. TO MARY WITH LOVE, Richard Sherman, *romance*
- 125. FEBRUARY HILL, Victoria Lincoln, *novel*
- 126. QUALITY, Cid Ricketts Sumner, *novel*
- 127. CHICAGO MURDERS, Sewell Peaslee Wright, editor, *true crime*
- 130. THE CINNAMON MURDER, Frances Crane, *mystery*
- 131. THE PEARL, John Steinbeck, *novel*
- 135. MAMA'S BANK ACCOUNT, Kathryn Forbes, *romance*
- 136. UP AT THE VILLA, W. Somerset Maugham, *novel*
- 139. STATION WEST, Luke Short, *Western*
- 140. CORONER CREEK, Luke Short, *Western*
- 141. THE SCANDALS OF CLOCHEMERLE, Gabriel Chevallier, *novel*
- 200. WESTERN TRIGGERS, Arnold Hano, editor, *anthology*
- 201. TRAIL SOUTH FROM POWDER VALLEY, Peter Field, *Western*
- 202. THE TENDERFOOT, W. H. B. Kent, *Western*
- 203. SUGARFOOT, Clarence Budington Kelland, *Western*
- 204. BLOOD ON THE MOON (*Gunman's Chance*), Luke Short, *Western*
- 206. DEPUTY MARSHAL, Charles Heckelmann, *Western*
- 227. AMERICAN SEXUAL BEHAVIOR AND THE KINSEY REPORT, Morris L. Ernst and David Loth, *non-fiction*
- 250. THE STAGLINE FEUD, Peter Dawson, *Western*
- 251. RELENTLESS (*Three Were Thoroughbreds*), Kenneth Perkins, *Western*
- 252. BARBED WIRE (*Powdersmoke Fence*), Bennett Foster, *Western*
- 253. WILD JUSTICE (*The Smoky Years*), Alan LeMay, *Western*
- 254. THE BORDER BANDIT, Evan Evans, *Western*

300. **THE KIDNAP MURDER CASE,** S. S. Van Dine, *mystery*
301. **HEADLINED FOR MURDER** (*Slug It Slay*), Edwin Lanham, *mystery*
302. **THE FABULOUS CLIPJOINT,** Fredric Brown, *mystery*
303. **SIREN IN THE NIGHT,** Leslie Ford, *mystery*
304. **THE PROBLEM OF THE WIRE CAGE,** John Dickson Carr, *mystery*
305. **HANGED FOR A SHEEP,** Frances & Richard Lockridge, *mystery*
307. **THE BRIDE SAW RED,** Robert Carson, *romance*
350. **YOUR RED WAGON** (*Thieves Like Us*), Edward Anderson, *novel*
351. **THE LYING LADIES,** Robert Finnegan, *mystery*
352. **MISS AGATHA DOUBLES FOR DEATH,** H. L. V. Fletcher, *mystery*
354. **SAN FRANCISCO MURDERS,** Joseph Henry Jackson, ed., *true crime*
355. **THE MAN WITHIN,** Graham Greene, *novel of suspense*
400. **WINTER MEETING,** Ethel Vance, *novel*
401. **YESTERDAY'S MADNESS,** Marian Cockrell, *romance*
402. **THE RED PONY,** John Steinbeck, *novel*
404. **HIROSHIMA,** John Hersey, *the story of six survivors*
405. **THE HUCKSTERS,** Frederic Wakeman, *novel*
406. **MICKEY** (*Clementine*), Peggy Goodin, *novel*
407. **BEHOLD THIS WOMAN,** David Goodis, *novel*
408. **DOCTOR KIM,** Lucy Agnes Hancock, *romance*
409. **LOW MAN ON A TOTEM POLE,** H. Allen Smith, *hilarious revelations*
450. **MOONLIT VOYAGE** (*The Moon to Play With*), Elizabeth Dunn, *romance*
451. **LOVE IS THE WINNER** (*Who Wins His Love*), Natalie Shipman, *romance*
452. **CABBAGE HOLIDAY,** Anthony Thorne, *novel*
453. **FIVE NIGHTS** (*Five Days*), Eric Hatch, *novel*
454. **THE CHINESE ROOM,** Vivian Connell, *novel*
455. **LOVE IS A SURPRISE** (*Letty and the Law*), Faith Baldwin, *romance*
456. **YANKEE STOREKEEPER,** R. E. Gould, *novel*
500. **MY GREATEST DAY IN BASEBALL,** John P. Carmichael, ed.
501. **STRIKEOUT STORY,** Bob Feller, *real, action-packed baseball*
502. **THE UNEXPECTED,** edited by Bennett Cerf, *anthology*
503. **FIRST LOVE,** Joseph Greene & Elizabeth Abell, editors, *short stories*
550. **MILTON'S BERLE'S JOKE BOOK** (*Out of My Trunk*)
552. **THE GASHOUSE GANG,** J. Roy Stockton, The St. Louis Cardinals
554. **HOT LEATHER** (*The Life of Jimmy Dolan*), Bertram Millhauser and Beulah Marie Dix, *novel of the prize ring*
205. **RED RIVER** (*Blazing Guns on the Chisholm Trail*), Borden Chase, *Western*
256. **WESTERN ROUNDUP,** ed. by Arnold Hano, *anthology*
306. **THE DAY HE DIED,** Lewis Padgett, *mystery*
356. **SORRY, WRONG NUMBER,** Allan Ullman & Lucille Fletcher, *novel of suspense*
403. **BEGGAR'S CHOICE,** George Axelrod, *novel*
458. **DR. WOODWARD'S AMBITION,** Elizabeth Seifert, *romance*
460. **EARTH AND HIGH HEAVEN,** Gwethalyn Graham, *novel*
504. **KICK-OFF!** Edward Fitzgerald, editor, *non-fiction football anthology*

Bantam Books, Inc., 1107 Broadway, N. Y. 10, N. Y.

A Special Offer to Bantam Book Readers

# "Out of Print" Best Sellers Sent Directly To Your Home

While they last, the famous books listed below can be obtained from Bantam Books, Inc., 1107 Broadway, New York 10. Each of them has enjoyed tremendous popularity. Each was a top-notch best-seller of its kind. Although officially out of print and out of circulation, a small quantity of these books is on reserve in our warehouse for Bantam readers. For each title send 25c plus 5c for postage and handling.

2. **THE GIFT HORSE,** by Frank Gruber
   A tough, fast, funny mystery starring Johnny Fletcher.
9. **ROGUE MALE,** by Geoffrey Household
   An exciting adventure of espionage.
10. **SOUTH MOON UNDER,** by Marjorie Kinnan Rawlings
    Exciting novel of life and love in the Florida swamps.
11. **MR. & MRS. CUGAT,** by Isabel Scott Rorick
    Laughs and romances of a married couple.
14. **WIND, SAND AND STARS,** by Antoine de Saint-Exupéry
    Famous story of adventure in the air. Illus.
15. **MEET ME IN ST. LOUIS,** by Sally Benson
    Humorous tintype of American family life.
20. **OIL FOR THE LAMPS OF CHINA,** by Alice Tisdale Hobart
    Love and courage in the fabulous East.
21. **MEN, WOMEN AND DOGS,** by James Thurber
    Hilarious cartoons.
29. **WAS IT MURDER?,** by James Hilton
    Fast-moving mystery by author of Good-Bye Mr. Chips.
30. **CITIZEN TOM PAINE,** by Howard Fast
    Fascinating historical novel about a famous revolutionary.
31. **THE THREE HOSTAGES,** by John Buchan
    Exciting spy story with intrigue, adventure and pursuit.
33. **THE PRISONER OF ZENDA,** by Anthony Hope
    Unforgettable romance about a man who played king.
35. **MY DEAR BELLA,** by Arthur Kober
    Two laughs per page of her adventures in the Bronx.
37. **DRAWN AND QUARTERED,** by Chas. Addams
    Hair-raising, side-splitting cartoons.
39. **LONG, LONG AGO,** by Alexander Woollcott
    Famous people and humorous anecdotes.
41. **DAVID HARUM,** by Edward Noyes Westcott
    Popular novel about a horse-trader who helps young love.

## *You can have these Superior Reprints, too*

**OL' MAN ADAM AN' HIS CHILLUN,** by Roark Bradford
"Green Pastures" was based on this delightful book.
**THE RYNOX MURDER MYSTERY,** by Philip MacDonald
Tops for puzzle, action and snappy dialogue.
**CARTOONS BY GEORGE PRICE**
220 funny cartoons, by one of America's best cartoonists.
**MURDER IN MINK,** by Robert George Dean
Tough story with gorgeous "gals" and hard-drinking detectives.
**THE LOVE NEST, & Other Stories,** by Ring Lardner
Includes some of Lardner's most famous short stories.
**THE NAVY COLT,** by Frank Gruber
Gun-fanciers, blackmailers, plug-uglies, and literary ladies.
**THE INFORMER,** by Liam O'Flaherty
The stirring, well-known novel of Ireland. Thrilling movie of the same title was based on this book.
**THIS GUN FOR HIRE,** by Graham Greene
A top-notch thriller by the author of "The Confidential Agent".
**ON ICE,** by Robert George Dean
A handful of beautiful diamonds meant—murder.
**THE MIGHTY BLOCKHEAD,** by Frank Gruber
By one of America's most entertaining mystery writers.
**THE SHE-WOLF AND OTHER STORIES,** by "Saki" (H. H. Munro)
Delightful, witty stories by the world-famous author.
**GOOD NIGHT SHERIFF,** by Harrison R. Steeves
A murder mystery that packs a punch.
**UNEXPECTED NIGHT,** by Elizabeth Daly
A mystery with a believable plot and characters who are human.
**THE HOUSE WITHOUT THE DOOR,** by Elizabeth Daly
A mystery that challenges untangling.
**FAMILY AFFAIR,** by Ione S. Shriber
The most bizarre and terrifying murder case of Lieutenant Grady's exciting career.
**INQUEST,** by Percival Wilde
Murder and comedy blended by an expert mystery writer.
**ONE FOOT IN HEAVEN,** by Hartzell Spence
Hilarious doings of a practical parson in and out of trouble.
**MR. ANGEL COMES ABOARD,** by C. G. Booth
Catastrophe in mid-ocean plunges a lovely girl into murder.
**WHITE MAGIC,** by Faith Baldwin
Three groups of people tangle in this romance on skis.
**AN APRIL AFTERNOON,** by Philip Wylie
Sparkling story of a love that violates conventions and laws.
**EMBARRASSMENT OF RICHES,** by Marjorie Fischer
Spine-tingling adventure of spies and intrigue.

For each book send 25c, plus 5c for postage and handling, to
**BANTAM BOOKS, Inc., 1107 Broadway, New York 10, N. Y.**